People in Period

TUDOR PEOPLE

JOHN FINES

West Sussex Institute of Higher Education, Chichester

B T Batsford Ltd *London*

For Carol and David

General Editor
Dr James L. Henderson
Institute of Education
University of London
and Chairman, The World Education
Fellowship.

First published 1977
© John Fines 1977

ISBN 0 7134 0283 0

Printed in Great Britain by
The Anchor Press Ltd, Tiptree, Essex,
for the publishers B T Batsford Ltd,
4 Fitzhardinge Street, London W1H 0AH

ACKNOWLEDGMENT

The Author and Publishers thank the following for their kind permission to reproduce copyright illustrations: The British Library for fig 6; Courtauld Institute of Art for figs 1, 2, 41, 51; Edinburgh University Library for figs 21, 32; India Office Library and Records for fig 43; Lamport Hall Preservation Trust Limited and English Life Publications Limited for fig 49; Lamport Hall Preservation Trust Limited and Northamptonshire Record Office for fig 42; The Mansell Collection for figs 24, 44, 47, 48; National Library of Ireland for fig 22; National Portrait Gallery for figs 16, 54; Photographie Giraudon for figs 14, 38, 39; Radio Times Hulton Picture Library for figs 3-5, 8-13, 15, 16, 18-20, 23, 25-31, 34-7, 40, 45, 46, 52, 53, 56-59; Victoria and Albert Museum for figs 50, 55.

Contents

Acknowledgment		2
List of illustrations		4
Introduction		5
1	THE SQUIRE: Sir Nathaniel Bacon of Stiffkey	7
2	THE DIARIST: Lady Margaret Hoby	13
3	THE SCHOOLBOY: as seen by Juan Luis Vives	18
4	THE COURTIER: Robert Carey	23
5	THE ADVENTURER: Sir Thomas Stucley	30
6	THE CHURCHMAN: Miles Coverdale	37
7	THE SOLDIER: William, Lord Grey of Wilton	43
8	THE MERCHANT ADVENTURER: John Isham	51
9	THE MUSICIAN: Thomas Wythorne	57
10	THREE CRIMINALS: Browne, Phillips and Fennor	63
List of dates		68
Book list		69
Index		71

List of illustrations

1 Nathaniel Bacon's father, Nicholas 7
2 Nicholas Bacon's family tree 8
3 Francis Bacon 9
4 Three witches: Joan Flower and her daughters 9
5 Tribunal of a king's bailiff 10
6 Lady Hoby's diary 16
7 Lady Hoby's mother-in-law 15
8 Elizabethan family at prayer 17
9 Schoolteacher and boys 19
10 Schoolteacher listening to a boy 20
11 Children at play 22
12 Presence Chamber at Hampton Court 23
13 English fire-ships 24
14 Siege of Rouen 26
15 Nonsuch Palace 28
16 Elizabeth I 29
17 Charles I 29
18 Robert Carey, Earl of Monmouth 29
19 Charles Brandon, Duke of Suffolk 30
20 Edward Seymour, Duke of Somerset 31
21 Tower of London 31
22 Map of Ulster 32
23 Philip II 33
24 Battle of Lepanto 34
25 Don Juan of Austria 34
26 Lisbon harbour 36
27 Thomas Cromwell 38
28 William Tyndale 38
29 Coverdale's Bible 39
30 Elizabeth I's copy of Coverdale's Bible 40
31 Latimer preaching 41
32 Bishop's vestments 42
33 Miles Coverdale 42
34 Firing a cannon 43
35 Town under siege 45
36 Calais from the sea 46
37 Aerial view of Calais 46
38 Queen Mary and King Philip 47
39 Duke of Guise 48
40 Mortars on movable carriages 48
41 Lord Grey 50
42 John Isham's account book 52
43 Procession passing Mercers' Hall 52
44 Market women and apprentice 53
45 Stock Exchange at Antwerp 53
46 Elizabethan merchant 54
47 Cloth hall and wool market at Chipping Campden 55
48 Flemish weaver 55
49 John Isham 56
50 Elizabeth I's virginal 58
51 Thomas Whythorne 58
52 Three musical ladies 59
53 Musical party 60
54 Thomas Whythorne 62
55 Elizabethan harpsichord 62
56 Forged passport 63
57 Ale house 64
58 Mary Frith, the infamous thief 66
59 Supper at an inn 67

Introduction

It is difficult to give any really accurate figures, but there were probably as many as four and a half million people living in England at the end of the sixteenth century. Maybe it was more, maybe it was less, but as they did not have a census office then we cannot know for sure. One thing, however, is certain — the people described in this book are only a handful of the many different kinds of people who lived in Tudor England. Many fascinating people have had to be left out, but there are numerous other books where you can find out about Tudor people, and it will be possible for you to write some biographies of your own later. A very good start is to find the *Dictionary of National Biography* in the public library. It is a large work in many volumes, but any reader who wants to know about famous and not so famous people in Tudor times will find short biographies there.

This book tries to cover a fairly wide range of types of people. They have been chosen from the second ranks of history — that is the ranks of the 'not quite so famous' who do not often figure in normal textbooks. This does not mean that they were not interesting or not important. Indeed, it is often these kinds of people who can tell you most about the times they lived in. Famous people are rarely typical of their age; often we say of them, 'There was a man born before his time' or 'He stood head and shoulders above his own generation'. Leonardo da Vinci invented a form of flying machine hundreds of years before the Wright brothers got theirs off the ground and so we admire him greatly and call him a genius; but he was the only man of his day who could have done such a thing or was concerned enough to do so.

The second reason for choosing the people who appear in this book is that they wrote a fair amount of material themselves, or their contemporaries wrote about them. All these characters have been reconstructed from the documents they left behind. When you start to look for documents about people in the past, you will be amazed how much survives. It is a little miracle that Lady Hoby's diary has survived for us to read, and what is specially nice is that it has been printed so that anyone who can use a public library can read it for themselves. There is so much material from Tudor times in print that anyone who can read can start to be a historian straight away.

Because all the people in this book are so different (although they lived in the same age, and in many cases met or were connected with one another in some way), the reader can start anywhere. It depends what you want to know about Tudor people. If you are interested in sea-dogs and pirates then you can begin with Sir Thomas Stucley. If you want to know about musicians, then Thomas Whythorne should be your first choice.

When you have started to read you will

find some facts that are interesting and useful for your own further study, and you should make a note of these. Also, many questions will be raised by your reading about issues you do not quite understand — points you want to look at further. It is well worth while writing these down, so that you can ask for the answers or look them up yourself.

In each of the biographies you will find references to dates, events and other people, some of whom are written about in other biographies in this book. To get all this clear in your mind, it is useful to build up a time chart so that you can see when Miles Coverdale lived in relation to Robert Carey or where the Duke of Somerset fits in with Thomas Stucley, Lord Grey and Thomas Whythorne. The Duke of Somerset is rather a confusing fellow, for he began his rise to fame with one title (the Earl of Hertford) and reached a peak with another (the Duke of Somerset). If you put him down on your time chart and then look up more details about him to add to it, you will find you begin to understand a lot more about the people in this book. Other people who might figure on the chart are the Tudor kings and queens of England.

When you are well into the book, you can start to use other books more thoroughly to build up a background to these people's lives. The turbulent northern border of England plays a large part in several of the biographies and it would be a good idea to find out more about this. The Court is also mentioned in many biographies, so why not find out details about life at Court from other books? The very tricky subject of religion also comes up here and there, so try to find other books that will tell you, for example, more about the Catholics who Sir Nathaniel Bacon was chasing (see p. 12).

After you have read the book and made your notes, built your time chart, searched in other books for the answers to your questions and the details of things that interest you, you should have learned a good deal about the people of Tudor England. You can do more, however. You can find a Tudor character who lived in your own area and make your own biography of him or her. Your public library will have a local history collection with county histories in it. The best might be the *Victoria County History*, but there are many different kinds. If you browse through the section on Tudor times you should soon find an interesting character, and quite a lot about him. The *Dictionary of National Biography* might provide some more information and there might be some surviving documents printed by your county record society or some other body. You can quickly check these by looking up your character in Conyers Read's *Bibliography of British History : Tudor Period* (2nd edn.), Oxford, 1959.

1 THE SQUIRE:

Sir Nathaniel Bacon of Stiffkey

Nathaniel was the second son of Sir Nicholas Bacon, one of the leading men in government in Queen Elizabeth's reign. His younger half-brother, Francis, was one of the greatest writers and philosophers England has produced. To have belonged to such a family must have been a great spur to success, but Nathaniel rose to a high position in his county of Norfolk by steady plodding. He studied law in London, entering Gray's Inn in 1562, and was a Member of Parliament six times between 1574 and 1604. He became Sheriff of Norfolk in 1599 and was knighted in 1604, 18 years before his death. However, it is as a Justice of the Peace that he is most interesting to historians.

As one might expect of a Justice of the Peace, Sir Nathaniel had much to do with the punishment of criminals in his area. He presided over serious cases such as murder, some of which presented as many complications as a modern detective story. For instance, on 21 October 1600, a merchant of King's Lynn told Nathaniel Bacon that about six years before, a sea captain had been to the Judge of the Admiralty for Norfolk and had testified that one of his crew had confessed to murdering a tall man at sea off the coast of King's Lynn. The supposed murderer had left the ship at Iceland, but the captain had described him to the judge in case he should return.

He did, and the judge called him to answer the charge. He pleaded guilty, was put in prison and no more was heard of him. Presumably the merchant then wanted the case to be reopened, but there seem to be no other references to it in Sir Nathaniel's papers, so perhaps he found it too baffling to cope with.

1   Nathaniel Bacon's father, Nicholas, holding his wand and seal of office.

2 *opposite* Nicholas Bacon's family tree. He sits at the bottom with his first wife on the left and his second on the right, and the tree grows upwards.

3 *right* Nathaniel's half-brother, Francis Bacon, the famous writer and philosopher, who became Viscount of St Albans.

Assault and battery usually presented fewer problems. Wife-stealing was rather complex and so were accusations of witchcraft. Agnes Ames was so accused, after a long squabble with her neighbours, the Cranes. It all began when the Cranes's servant, Elizabeth Mower, visited Mrs Ames's house to borrow a firebrand to light their fires. After she had gone Mrs Ames missed some of her spinning equipment and accused Elizabeth of stealing it. Elizabeth vigorously

4 Three witches: Joan Flower and her daughters, Margaret and Philippa. They were executed by burning.

denied the charge and Mrs Ames finally withdrew, but threatened vengeance. Three weeks later Elizabeth was taken ill with severe rheumatic pains. It was then that people recalled that years ago there had been tales of Agnes Ames magically curing her sick child and that she had once been friendly with a fortune-teller, who was said to have been taught his trade by a sorcerer. Mr Crane began to wonder whether his recent sleepless nights were the work of Agnes Ames. He also wondered whether she had been responsible for the strange illness of one of his cows and of one of his pigs. Mrs Ames held bread in her hands and solemnly swore that she was not a witch, but she had to go before the JP. Let us hope he dismissed the case quickly.

Most cases were genuine however and some were very sad, like that of the two mad women who tried to burn down the village of Wymondham, believing that afterwards they could escape abroad and the Pope would reward them. Now, such people would be put into hospital to be cured of mental delusions, but at least one of these two ladies was executed. Some of the rogues who appear in Sir Nathaniel's papers should have been executed but were not. The worst of these was John Ferrour, a money lender. He was a wicked old man who managed to charge enormous interest on his loans by making the interest payable to his step-daughter, so that it looked as though he was getting only his loan back. He lent a person called Henry Laborne £5 for six months and his step-daughter received a 'gift' of a piece of land worth £1 a year. When Laborne wanted to pay back the loan, Ferrour refused on some technical grounds. Thus, the loan was renewed and the step-daughter was given a substantial load of barley this time. At the end of that year, Laborne was forced to agree to pay Ferrour £1 10s a year for the rest of their lives. The old skinflint even behaved despicably to his family, so disliking children that when the schoolmaster brought Ferrour's grandchild to his home to avoid the rain, he

had the schoolmaster arrested for trespass and the poor man was forced to go to London to disentangle the case.

The JP also had to supervise other officers of the law and see that they carried out their jobs properly. Occasionally he met with complaints, some of which were perfectly justified. A man called Pigeon brought a case against Thomas Watts, and when the bailiffs went to arrest Watts he refused them entry. Though old and bedridden and very fat, he did not lack courage; nor did his sons who

5   A bailiwick or tribunal of a king's bailiff. While the bailiff tries the case, his secretary take notes, and a queue of plaintiffs waits outside.

fought the bailiffs while his daughter-in-law, Grace, and her maid biffed them with spits, hurled stones and set the dog on them. Eventually, the bailiffs broke down a portion of the wall and carried Thomas out. They put him on two old feather beds in a cart to take him to London. Nothing would stop them — pleas, threats or bribes — and when the old man died on arrival at the Fleet prison in London, the warden hastily claimed that it was the journey that had killed him and an enquiry was set up.

Crime took up much of Sir Nathaniel's time, but he had many other duties as well. He was greatly concerned with fostering local trade. For example, he checked that not too many of Norfolk's vital supplies were exported. He also had to supervise the patents and monopolies authorized by the Queen, whereby one man was granted the right to supply one area with one type of merchandise for a certain period of time, totally without competition, in return for a substantial payment. The man who held the salt monopoly caused a considerable problem to Sir Nathaniel. Often there was just no salt and, along with many others, he must have frequently cursed the monopolies system.

Sir Nathaniel also had to supervise the alehouses (a tricky job in those days, even though the penalties for serving bad beer or giving short measure were commendably stiff) and overlook the work of the surveyors of the highways. He was on the commission that dealt with the sea defences and the drainage dykes of the area. This was a great problem, for sea walls cost more than the community could willingly afford, even though they knew that a flood would cost them much more still. Sometimes, the sea soaked up too much money, as when Sir Nathaniel built his expensive pier at Cromer, to make the loading and unloading of cargoes easier. At other times, the sea threw wealth back onto the land, in the form of goods from wrecked ships. Local people often regarded these as 'pennies from heaven' and

tried to take what they found, but Sir Nathaniel worked hard to enforce the law. He received reports of pieces of wood, small boats, hatches, staves, pikes and wine barrels that had come ashore. Often these barrels were empty by the time the report was made, though it is questionable whether they were empty when they came ashore.

The local juries also worked as coroners' juries. One sad tale brought before them was that of a boy of 17 who, while playing in a mill, had got caught in the machinery and horribly injured. In fact, there were so many sad tales of this kind coming before Sir Nathaniel that he must often have shaken his head over his papers and wondered what the world was coming to.

Much of Sir Nathaniel's business presented him with problems. For instance, he had to collect taxes, loans and subsidies and he had to supervise the new Poor Law. This was a harsh law, which allowed poor people to be helped only in their place of birth. If they travelled in search of work, they would find themselves out of reach of help. When a poor boy of ten or 12 lay sick of a fever in Warham, Sir Nathaniel ordered his removal to his birthplace; he died in the cart on the way there and, on arrival, his body was dumped outside the constable's door. Sir Nathaniel was very concerned that he had not been told how ill the boy was and that the constable of Warham had been so heartless as to pack him off in a cart in such a weak state of health.

These were hard times indeed, but they were harder still when war threatened. Sir Nathaniel had to make lists of the ships and their crews on the coast of Norfolk and supervise the pressing of men into the navy in the period before the Armada (1588). He was also in charge of the muster, making sure that the county produced its fair quota of men, horses, weapons, gunpowder, armour and money for the army on active service. It was hard work to get people to pay their allotted share, to keep the powder dry and the equipment in good order. The government kept demanding more, and Sir Nathaniel's position was that of the man in the middle.

Most people will think that this was enough for one man to do, and more, but as a Justice of the Peace and a Member of Parliament Sir Nathaniel had many other jobs thrust upon him by the Queen's Council in London. If he did not do them well he was soon reprimanded. Perhaps the most difficult of his other tasks was keeping control of the religious matters in his area. In the last years of Queen Elizabeth's reign, religion was as touchy a subject as at any time in English history. There were many Protestant extremists who wanted to change the Church rapidly, expelling the bishops and replacing the elaborate ceremonies with simple meetings. On the other hand, there were still many Catholics in England, despite the strict laws discriminating against them, and Jesuit priests travelled round the country in disguise holding services for them. Jesuit priests took a big risk because if they were caught they would suffer torture and execution. The country gentleman who, like Sir Nathaniel, was a JP, MP and sheriff by turn, had to try to enforce the laws against both extremes and keep people firmly in the middle of the road. An example of his work can be found in a letter of about 1597, written by a man sent to look for a Roman Catholic priest called Upton. He had been ordered to search Francis Woodhouse's house at Breckles, and was annoyed to find, when he got there after a 28-mile journey, that

Woodhouse had moved. But the searcher plodded on to Woodhouse's new address at Caston, a mile and a half away, no doubt cursing Sir Nathaniel for having given him an out-of-date address. Mr Woodhouse was out hawking, but the searcher got down to work and soon discovered two rosaries (the beads which Catholics use to keep count of their prayers) and some books, pictures and objects he thought to be 'popish'. When Mr Woodhouse returned the searcher took from him the keys of the old house at Breckles. There he caught a Lincolnshire man called Wilkinson, a great traveller whom he strongly suspected of being a Catholic priest, a visitor called Hubberd who claimed he had come to see his father-in-law, Mr Fludde, about a sparrowhawk, and an old lady, who was very 'popish' and was kept by Mrs Woodhouse. The searcher went on to examine Fludde's house, for he suspected him as well, and as usual he read all the letters and papers he could find. He prodded around the outhouses, which were full of corn, thinking a priest might be hidden there, but he couldn't find any trace of Upton. He reported that he had arrested nobody, but noted that if Sir Nathaniel wanted it, he could arrest them easily at any time. There was no privacy or freedom in Tudor England.

Therefore, as MP, JP and sheriff, Sir Nathaniel Bacon had many difficult and unpleasant duties to discharge and responsibility weighed heavily on his shoulders. He devoted his life to his county of Norfolk and, although at times he might have seemed harsh and cruel, he was a just and honest man.

2 THE DIARIST:
Lady Margaret Hoby

Keeping a diary has made lots of people famous. In particular, Samuel Pepys and John Evelyn, who lived in the period after the one we are studying, won great fame from their diaries. Lady Margaret Hoby kept a diary from 1599 to 1605, and she must have been one of the earliest Englishwomen to keep a regular diary. It tells us a great deal about the life of a remarkable woman who, by chance, was connected with many of the other people who appear in this book.

Margaret was born into the Dakins family, in the East Riding of Yorkshire, in about 1571. Her family were quite well off. Most of them had made a lot of money from land which was very cheaply obtained in the years after the monasteries were closed by Henry VIII. We know little of Margaret's parents apart from their wealth and influence (her father was a JP, like Sir Nathaniel Bacon), for they sent her early on in her life to be brought up in another household. As a rich girl who would win many keen suitors, Margaret needed to learn how to behave in the big world of high society and, more important, she needed to make influential friends.

So she was sent to live in the household of Catherine, Countess of Huntingdon, who already had a large number of boys and girls from various homes to bring up — it was like a small public school. Catherine was a very strict person and deeply religious, favouring the more extreme Puritanism. She thought a lot about the sins of man and carefully avoided all those things she called 'worldly' — cards, strong drink, popular music, dancing (although it is one of the oddities of our story that Catherine's mother, the Duchess of Northumberland, tried to get Thomas Whythorne to teach her daughter music). In their place she put prayer meetings, Bible reading and attending sermons. Perhaps it sounds dull, but we must remember that many Tudor people found life to be good, and enjoyed it. One of these was Margaret Dakins.

When Margaret had received sufficient training in household and estate management, the use of medicines and surgery, and had learned to read and write, she was reckoned to be ready for marriage. She was 20 by then, which was somewhat late for marriage by Tudor standards. A suit was arranged with Walter Devereux, son of the Earl of Essex and brother of Robert, Queen Elizabeth's favourite. (She had no say whatsoever in her first two marriages.) He was a much loved person and had himself been brought up by the Countess of Huntingdon, so he must have known Margaret well. He was probably very pleased with the marriage agreement : an estate was purchased for the newly-weds at Hackness, near Scarborough, towards which Mr Dakins paid £3,000 and the Earl of Essex contributed the same amount. The Earl of Huntingdon made up the difference in the total price with the final payment of £500. Having patrons like the Huntingdon family really did pay!

The young couple must have thought that they had every chance of happiness, but within two years Walter was killed at the siege of Rouen, where Robert Carey (see p.25) was a captain. We do not know how much Margaret grieved for him, but she was given very little time to do so, for within a fortnight a strange undersized fellow with the oddest of names was vigorously courting her — this was Thomas Posthumous Hoby.

Thomas was called 'Posthumous' because he was born shortly after the death of his father, an able diplomat. His mother Elizabeth, a somewhat daunting person, had therefore had a very great influence on his life. She was one of the daughters of Sir Anthony Cooke, who believed strongly in the education of girls : one of her sisters married William Cecil, who was to become Lord Burghley, whilst another married Sir Nicholas Bacon, father of the famous Francis and of our Sir Nathaniel (see p. 7). Elizabeth first married Sir Thomas Hoby and then John Lord Russell, son of the Earl of Bedford. Interestingly, Lord Russell's sisters married

6   *opposite* A page from Lady Hoby's diary. It is well written, but the handwriting and the spelling are strange to us.

the Earl of Cumberland, who accompanied Carey (see p. 23) on some of his adventures, and Ambrose Dudley, whom we meet briefly in Thomas Whythorne's story (see p.60).

Lady Russell was a difficult person. She was always taking issue with her neighbours and when she did not approve of the judicial decisions she took the law into her own hands. She even kept a pair of stocks in her courtyard for punishing wrongdoers. Thomas behaved like her in later life, but as a youngster he never got on with her, although she self-righteously claimed that she had spent £7,000 on his upbringing. He was small and sickly, and often taunted. People called him 'scurvy urchin' and 'spindle-shanked ape', and spread rumours to the effect that he put on his breeches with a shoe-horn. His mother sent him to study law in London, when he was still almost a boy but all the other students were young men. He ran away, claiming that he would learn more travelling abroad, like his brother. His mother appealed to William Cecil to take him over and it seems he did take charge of this unpleasing and rebellious boy, for it was Cecil who wrote to Mr Dakins about a marriage between Thomas Hoby and Margaret within a fortnight of Walter Devereux's death. However, even the Lord Treasurer of England, Queen Elizabeth's chief minister, had proved too slow. The Countess of Huntingdon, no doubt remembering her investment of £500 in Hackness, had already fixed a new marriage between Margaret and her nephew Thomas Sidney, brother of Sir Philip. You can imagine how cross Thomas Hoby's mother was. She had promised him £500 a year if he man-

The Lady Hobbei.

7   Lady Hoby's mother-in-law in her younger days. She does not look as fierce as people found her to be.

Wensday
the 21:
After priuat praier I went into the garden and after I
had walked I wrought and talked with som strangers that
came to se me till dinner time after dinner I wrought and
hard Mr: Rhodes Read till allmost supper time then I
tooke a Lector medetated and praied and so went to
supper after I hard a Lector and then walked a whill
and then went to praier and so to bed:

Thursday
the 22:
After priuat praier I writt in my sarmon booke
then I walked and dined and after that till night
I wrought then I praied with Mr: Rhodes and
then hard a Lector and so went to supper after
I writt a letter to my Cosine Isons and praied
priuatly and so went to bed:

Friday
the 23:
After priuat praier I writt notes in my testement and
then eate my breakfast after I praied and then dined
after that I did sum more busenesse and then I took
a Lector and after that praied and examined my selfe
after that to supper then to the Lector and so to bed:

Saterday
the 24:
After priuat praiers I did eate my breakfast and then
writt of my sarmon book then I walked read of the bible
praied and so went to dinner after dinner I tooke or
der for thinges about the house praied bills medeta
ted and praied and so went to the Lector then to
supper after I walked and talked with Mr: Rhodes
read of the bible and after praied and then went
to bed:

The Lords
day 25:
After priuat I went to church after I praied then
to dinner then I some after to church then I talked
with my maides of taretaynes their deliuered and
then I hard Mr: Lauighret Rhodes read of Mr: Greshā
ine after that I examined my selfe and praied
and some after that to supper then to publike praiers
after that to priuat and so to bed:

aged to marry this rich heiress and had even suggested that he should try to elope with her.

Thomas did not try eloping. He waited, and four years later, in 1595, Sidney died. Within a week, Thomas, now a knight, had started his campaign. He pestered everyone with the slightest bit of influence to write to Margaret in his favour, and he travelled to see her with presents of jewels and pearls. She clearly was not very impressed by this eager, runtish little fellow and tried hard to put him off, protesting that her grief for Sidney made it impossible for her to think of a new husband. However, Thomas persisted and eventually won through when Margaret suddenly found herself facing a court case that threatened her control of Hackness. She knew then she needed a husband with influence, and one who knew how the law worked.

They were married in August 1596. There was no great ceremony, just dinner and a sermon, for both were strong Puritans and disliked dancing and music. Then they went north to settle at Hackness. Most of their neighbours were Catholics, rough and ready Yorkshiremen who thought much of physical strength and found the law complicated and dangerous. They were not pleased to have Sir Thomas Hoby arrived in their midst as JP and chief officer of the government in the district. He was the last sort of person they wanted: he was a Protestant, physically weak and addicted to the law. They said he was 'the sauciest little Jack in all the country and would have his oar in anybody's boat', and claimed that the Yorkshire lads would show him a trick or two, which would have him down in the end.

Margaret got on with the running of the house while Thomas was busy on commissions or in Parliament. It was a big job: she had ten male servants and four females, three of whom were widows taken in as an act of charity. Like the Countess of Huntingdon, Margaret also took in girls who wanted some education and wanted to improve their manners, and would help with some of the household duties. The following adapted extract from Margaret's diary shows how a fairly typical period in her life was spent:
Friday. Prayer, then wrote up notes of the

reading from a Holy book the night before. Out for a walk and talked of pleasant things. Home and wrote up last Sunday's sermon. To prayer again, and then dinner. Talked with friends, and played bowls. Back to the house and worked until four o'clock. Then prayed with my chaplain. Another walk, then more prayer. To supper, and after to hear the reading. To bed. . .

Monday. Prayer followed by housework, then breakfast. To church with Mr Hoby. Then home and to work without praying. Much troubled — felt ill, and considered it a judgement of God. After lunch, walked a little with Mr Hoby, after which he went off. Went to collect the apples due as part of the tithe payments. After getting home, prayed with the chaplain and on my own, examining my conscience. Walked before supper. Read then went to bed. . .

Thursday. In the morning, after prayer, wrote down household accounts. Then breakfast, and after some time looked into the good ordering of the granary. Mr Hoby returned for a short period, and I left off work to keep him company. After lunch, to see one of the villagers who was not very well, and to collect his tithe apples. Home and worked until six, when prayed with chaplain and meditated. To supper, a reading and then bed. . .

Friday. Much distressed that my drowsiness prevented me from properly meditating on the sermon that day. . .

Sunday. Prayer then to church, and on the way home gave thanks for such a good minister. After lunch, walked with Mr Hoby and then to church again. Called in on a poor man with a bad leg to see what help I could offer. Walked and read a sermon as I walked. Examined my conscience. To supper, then busy with Mr Hoby over paper work until prayers, then to bed.

Monday. Prayer, then went down to see to the dressing of the poor man's leg. Arranged

the housework with the servants and set to until dinner time. After lunch, spent the afternoon indoors reading a book on herbal remedies. Then visited my mother in my coach. Home to supper. Examined my conscience and joined the public prayers held in the hall, and to bed.

Tuesday. After breakfast, took my coach and visited Lady Eure, for two hours. Then on to see a cousin, and finally back to my mother's. Supper, prayers then bed.

Wednesday. After prayer and breakfast, took my coach and went on to York where I joined a jolly party of friends at Mr Scudamore's house. Later, I was sick during prayers and wondered whether I hadn't sinned earlier in the day forgetfully enjoying myself; the sickness was clearly God's punishment.

Thursday. To see a cousin and attend service in her house, followed by lunch. Went out in her coach to take the air, then back to her house for another service and supper.

Friday. Prayer, breakfast and to interview a new doctor I hoped would replace the unsatisfactory one I have. After lunch, quite a crowd of gentlewomen came round to talk with Mr Fuller on matters of religion. On to see a cousin who was about to have a baby. To supper with Mr Scudamore, and gave him money to cover the cost of the entertainment he had given whilst I was in York. After supper so many visitors came there was no time for formal public prayers, so prayed privately, and to bed.

Such was the life of Lady Hoby, at home and on her travels; it was a most religious and careful life. Most of it was carefully written down in her diary in neat and pleasant handwriting. She was obviously well loved, with many friends. Her third husband missed her most of all when she died in 1633. He dedicated a chapel to her memory, named St Margaret's, and seven years later when he came to make his will he spoke lovingly of the tiny portrait of her that was set in a gold bangle he constantly wore on his arm.

8 *opposite* **An Elizabethan family at prayer.**

3 THE SCHOOLBOY:

as seen by the schoolmaster Juan Luis Vives

Five o'clock in the morning and a noisy maid-servant comes into the room, shouting to the children to wake up. She opens the shutters and the glass windows, brushes the heavy clothes vigorously and then turns to brush and polish the children's shoes. The boys groan and grumble from bed that their eyes are full of sand, or so tightly shut that the maid will have to send for a locksmith to open them. Miserably, they get up and begin to dress — wearing underclothes in winter for warmth, not for cleanliness as we do. They were well used to fleas and bugs and lice, and changed their clothes only when they looked dirty, not when they really needed to. A boy would make a shirt last six days.

The maid tried to get some feeling for cleanliness: the hair should be combed 40 times, first with the thin teeth of the comb to untangle it and rid it of any residents, and then with the thick teeth to make it lie flat and neat. The children should carefully wash their mouths out (they used tooth-picks regularly at meals, so they did not need to brush their teeth) and scrub their hands and faces, paying special attention to washing their eyes and behind their ears. The children would make a pretence of washing, and try to claim that dirt was just wrinkled skin or patches discoloured by the sun, until the maid had a go at them herself. She took a last look at them, tucked handkerchieves in their belts, and then they said their morning prayer before leaving the bedroom. It was now time to greet the family. This was a formal affair, as in Tudor times parents felt it important to keep a distance from their children. Even so, they still managed to get involved. If the parents had been having a row, the mother would hope that her son would side with her, but he would feel too afraid of his father to do so. As a result, he would be out of favour with his mother for several days.

Children started school when they were about seven years of age. In Tudor times adulthood could come as early as 12, but more usually at 15, when a boy was ready for university or even the battlefield. The boy's father would try to explain to him, when he started school, what it was for: at the moment, he would say, you are nothing but a rough animal, but now a great artist (the teacher) will take you into his laboratory (the school) to turn you into a human being. It would cost from as little as 1p. a week to as much as 5p. (which was expensive in those days); but it was worth it to learn Latin of the most correct kind (just as it was written by the finest writers of ancient days) and possibly also Greek and Hebrew. In the school library was a great pile of old books written in the Middle Ages, when people had forgotten how to write well: these were ready to be thrown out, for the boys were only to read pure Latin. They had to speak it too, all the time, or they would get the cane; it was the mark of the gentleman and

turned to the poets of the Middle Ages to find love songs, and soon spoilt his Latin that way. They also felt sorry for boys who were withdrawn by their shopkeeper fathers to learn more practical subjects such as French and mathematics. They were sorriest of all, though, for the poor beggar children who had no proper school. Their fate was a school like that set up in 1585 by Mr Wotton, an early Fagin (if you want to know more about Fagin, read *Oliver Twist* by Charles Dickens). He hung tiny bells, normally used in church or for hawking, around a pocket and a purse and taught the boys to take a counter from the pocket without making the bells ring. He who succeeded with the pocket was called a 'publique Foyster' and he who took silently from the purse was named a 'Judiciall Nypper' — so they had their schools, and we get from them the term 'nipper'.

The schools we are concerned with, however, were hoping to teach virtue, not vice. They were very anxious to bring up children well-mannered and obedient. One look at the wild vagabond children in the streets, totally out of control, told the better-off adults of the day how important it was to make their own children nicely behaved and absolutely obedient. To achieve this aim they indulged freely in corporal punishment. In the streets of London would be heard the cry, 'Buy my fine Jemmies! Buy my London tarters!' and the real indignity of it all was that children were made to buy the canes that were used on them both by their parents and their teachers. When Sir Peter Carrew ran away from school and threatened to throw himself from a high tower rather than give himself up to his teacher, his father had him leashed to a hound and chained him with it in the dog-kennel until he found means to make his escape. However, this was an age of violence and pain — there were no anaesthetics, few

scholar, and anyone who spoke good classical Latin could tour the known world and communicate freely wherever he went.

The boys were sorry for people who fell from the high standards they aimed at — characters like Clodius, who fell in love and medicines, little real comfort — so people didn't receive pain and indignity in the same way that we would today. Certainly the adults didn't consider themselves to be sadists; they believed sincerely in the vast majority of cases that they were doing children good, saving them from sin and damnation to hell. Education in Tudor times was very religious and people believed in angels and in devils, in heaven and in hell.

Our boy goes off to school then, taking with him a little snack of bread and butter

10　**This London teacher seems to be keen on using his birch. Notice how he listens to one boy reading whilst the rest get on with their work.**

and fruit to eat in the break time (nine to nine-fifteen). Meanwhile it is morning service at six o'clock, followed by an interview with the schoolmaster before proper school begins: the master is a worthy man, earning some £15 a year (more than the average vicar) and his usher, the assistant teacher is paid £9. The boy takes off his cap and bows his right knee before the man who will turn him into 'a man from a beast, a fruitful and good creature out of a useless one'.

The first lesson is reading: the boy must stand up straight before the usher, his cap under his left arm and his ABC tablet in his left hand. He must listen as his teacher pronounces each letter; then he must say them after him and point with a pointer to the letter being said on his tablet. He then goes to his seat and practises quietly, but not for long: in Tudor times children were expected to learn very quickly, and failure was not readily tolerated.

Writing comes next and the first art to be learnt is how to make a pen with a hen or goose quill. First you had to take a penknife (we still call it that, although we don't use it for the same purpose) and strip off all the little feathers near the point. Then you had to trim the top so that it wouldn't tickle your nose as you wrote. To smooth and shine the shank of the pen you used spit and polish, rubbing it vigorously on your jacket. Then the point of the quill was split into two and the top part was notched and trimmed so that both points were nearly equal (the right hand one, which you pressed on, could be a little longer). Now you were ready to write, using three fingers for a good neat copy, and thumb and forefinger for fast writing. The ink was kept in a little lead ink-well and was diluted with drops of water or vinegar if too thick. Even so, the writer needed to have a little sponge and his knife at the ready, to deal with excess ink on his pen. The paper had to be extra fine — the kind sold at 2½d (1p) a block — and the boys needed blotting paper, not to blot their work (that made the letters appear thin and ghostly) but to rest their hands on as they wrote so as not to smudge the page. The master's copy seemed so fair that they would groan a little when he gave it to them to copy six times, reminding them that the bodies of all their letters should be given an equal space, that they should join up all tailed letters (but not the round ones – p, o and b) and that they should split words at the end of lines by syllables, and not just any old how.

The boys would be glad when the morning ended (with prayers again) at 11 o'clock and they could go to lunch – soup, then meat with pickles and turnips or rice, and water, weak beer, or wine and water to drink. On holy days they had bread, fish and peas instead. Then there would be time to play a little or to stroll in the market, where they would be cheeky to the women who kept the stalls and try to steal their fruit.

School began again at one o'clock, with perhaps some music lessons and possibly some French, and probably also some more reading and writing of Latin. There was a break in some schools at three or three-thirty, and they finished with prayers once more at five or five-thirty. There was homework as well and, although there were half-day holidays most weeks, the main holidays of the year were rarely more than three vacations of a fortnight or under.

There was a little time after school for a game, before the six o'clock meal. But you had to be careful with whom you played – there were villains and cheats who stole your books and sold them, and cunning players who won from you your points (the little tags Tudor children used to keep their clothing joined in the middle, and which they were reduced to playing for when out of ready cash, not thinking how they would keep decent if they lost). There were also bullies and tell-tales to avoid, boys who spat on your page and trampled on your cap. With their good companions Tudor boys played a kind of marbles that involved throwing nuts into a hole, the one who got the most in taking the lot. There were also dice, draughts and card games. They argued as modern children do, and accused each other of 'not playing seriously', and when the maid came to say it was time for dinner there were cries of 'Now just as we are getting started she talks of stopping'. Some rich boys carried watches.

School dinner in boarding school was quite a splendid affair, with a feast master, chosen from the boys, to preside; there was a different one each week. They would lay a table-cloth and napkins, and polish up the silver, especially the big salt-cellar. Before starting their meal, they had to scrape the bread, which often came from the baker's with ash or even coal sticking to it. They had a pan of coals out on the table to keep the sauce hot and then, after grace, they would have a salad, a mutton stew cooked with prunes, root vegetables and herbs, or perhaps a pie, with cheese and fruit to follow. On holy days, they had fish, eggs and nuts. The boys ate with their caps on to keep their long hair out of the dishes and they also rolled up their sleeves, for they ate with fingers and a knife in a somewhat messy way. They needed their napkins. At the end of the meal, they would clean their knives and put them in their sheaths again, pick their teeth, say grace and clear away.

Just a little time left now to play, but then there was homework to be done for the next day. The Tudor schoolboy cost his parents a lot of money in candles and lamp-oil, although it was not the midnight oil he burned or he would never have been able to get up so early. He was in bed at eight o'clock in the winter and nine in the summer.

11 *Overleaf.* **A group of children at play. Some have toys, others have different kinds of bow, and the rest are tormenting an old man.**

4 THE COURTIER:

Robert Carey

Robert Carey was the youngest son of Lord Hunsdon, who was the son of Mary Boleyn and therefore cousin to Queen Elizabeth I. Robert was born in about 1560, right at the start of Elizabeth's reign, and he was probably first brought up at Court, but in 1568 his father was made warden of the East March and Robert's life changed greatly. The three Marches — the East, Middle and West March — were the border counties between England and Scotland. They had seen hundreds of years of theft, murder and vandalism, as men on each side of the border felt they had the right to do what they liked on the other side. Lord Hunsdon was a bluff, soldierly figure, and he very much enjoyed keeping order in this wild land.

Robert was placed in the care of tutors and governors, but he confesses in his autobiography that he had no natural ability for learning and he probably found riding around the harum-scarum wild-west land that his father ruled much more fun. By 1578, he was old enough to go to Court, and in the same year he was sent on embassy to the Netherlands. In 1582, he was back on the Continent, where he spent an agreeable nine months in Paris learning how to

12 **A fine scene of entertainment in the Presence Chamber at Hampton Court, during its great days.**

dress in the height of fashion, and lots more, no doubt. He was quite cross when his father (now Lord Chamberlain to the Queen), anxious about relations between England and France, ordered him to return home for his own safety.

In 1583, Robert Carey accompanied an ambassador to Scotland, where he met James VI, King of Scotland and heir to the English throne. They got on well, and James wrote to Elizabeth to ask whether the young man could spend some time at his Court. At first she agreed, and he was packed and ready to go from Berwick when an urgent message came from the Queen that she had changed her mind and he was to return to Court. Carey got used to this kind of behaviour during the next few years, but it

must have annoyed him intensely at first.

He was plainly much valued at Court and the following year, when the Queen's favourite — the Earl of Essex — stole away to go to the siege of Sluys, she sent Robert Carey to bring him back. Such were his powers of persuasion that, when he caught up with Essex at Sandwich, he got him to return to Court on his own, whilst Carey took his place in the adventure. In 1586, he was back at Court, much needed for a tricky job. The execution of Mary Queen of Scots was a difficult and delicate matter for Elizabeth to explain to Mary's son, James, so Carey was chosen to take letters to Scotland assuring the King of Elizabeth's innocence of this deed. James heard of Carey's mission and to prevent his being lynched in Scotland, where feelings were running high, he had two gentlemen meet him at the border to receive the Queen's letters. Such was the goodwill between the two, that Carey was Elizabeth's ambassador to James in the following year as well, and would have been again in 1588 had he not been ill.

This, of course, was the year of the great Armada, and as soon as Carey heard of it he and a friend hurried to Portsmouth where they ordered a frigate to take them out to sea. They experienced one of the hazards of naval warfare in the days before radio and radar — for a day they searched without being able to find the fleets. Then suddenly they were in the middle of the Spanish battle formation, and had to tack quickly back to join the British fleet. There they went on board the flagship, but they found it too crowded and so they put themselves aboard the *Elizabeth Bonaventure* as volunteers. They watched the fire-ships sail into the Armada at Calais, saw the Spaniards cut their anchors in their hurry to escape and looked on while men miserably waded ashore from the ship that got stranded. The battle continued — 'a cruel fight' Carey called it — until the English were out of ammunition. Then Carey landed near the Downs and went straight to Tilbury camp, where the Queen was. But he had caught a fever, and was carried away on a litter, dreadfully ill.

As the youngest son of a family of ten, Robert had little money and few expectations, but as he himself confesses, he lived well at Court, never stinting himself or his friends. So he got quickly into debt and, in 1589, having recovered from his fever, accepted a bet for £2,000 that he could not walk to Berwick in 12 days. Now that means covering 28 miles a day, often rough walking, but he was obviously desperate for the money for he won the bet.

In 1591, Robert lost a lot of that money accompanying the Earl of Essex to France to help Henry of Navarre fight the rebels there. He had 150 men to lead. His baggage was put in a cart with a team of five horses and he had to take five war horses as well. The cost of food was £30 a week, which was a great deal of money in those days, so obviously he entertained largely. In the middle of the campaign, Elizabeth — as might have been expected — recalled Essex. He did not want to go, and sent Carey to plead for him. Carey's counsellors all warned him not to do so, as it would make the Queen angry with him, but he went ahead and braved her wrath, explaining that Essex felt he would be thought a coward if he left the fight at this stage, and that this 'doom' would break his heart and shorten his life. These were wise arguments and Carey was so successful that the grateful Essex knighted him (although it was against the rules for him to do so). They continued besieging Rouen, and there poor Robert lost all his shirts in a night attack. Ever a dressy man, he had a large wardrobe, and when the order was given that all should wear shirts over their armour so that the English could recognize one another, everyone came to Carey to borrow a shirt. The attack failed, and the wardrobe stood empty.

When he returned home Elizabeth gave Carey £2,000 to settle his debts and he was offered the post of deputy warden of the West March. He enjoyed the work greatly, and proved that he could keep a firm hand over the violent border people. He married, surely for love for it was against everyone's advice and particularly annoyed the Queen, who liked to arrange her courtiers' marriages. Having lost the Queen's favour, Carey became very low in spirit and was soon deep in debt again. Apart from his father, the family were no help and behaved very badly to him. One tried to cheat him of a manor that should have been his, while another tried to prevent him taking up the post of warden of Norham castle, which again was his by right.

In 1593, Carey decided to try to win his way back into favour at Court. He spent £400 on his trappings and a present for the Queen and attended the ceremony that was held each year to commemorate her accession day. He dressed himself as 'the forsaken knight' who had sworn himself to a solitary life but could not resist paying tribute to his Queen. Everyone clearly knew who it was, including Elizabeth, but she was not that easily won. James of Scotland had recently asked for one of the Careys to be sent to him as a messenger, so she suggested that Robert should go, while still refusing to see him. He demanded that she should at least sign a safe-conduct pass as proof that she had really sent him; he then spurred his horse northwards.

In Scotland, James wished to give a verbal message, but again Carey demanded it in writing — he was too wise to take risks. He rushed back south and arrived at Hampton Court on Boxing Day. He went in straight away, without bothering to clean up, but found the Court holding a dance and the Queen in retirement in her inner rooms. His father went to announce him and Elizabeth said that Lord Hunsdon should bring in the papers. At that, Robert dug his toes in — he would see the Queen or not deliver the message. So he won his way back into the royal presence and into Elizabeth's favour once more.

Carey now took over from his father as warden of the East March, and quickly discovered the difficulties of the job he had inherited. Sir Robert Kerr, the Scottish warden and his opposite number, welcomed Carey to the post by raiding the East March and committing a brutal murder. Carey was determined not to be beaten and set to with

a hard policy of hanging every murderer and thief he could catch. Local gentry warned him that Sir Robert Kerr would take vengeance, especially when Carey captured Kerr's good friend, a man called Geordie Bourne, a murderer seven times over. Carey hung him, like the rest, and won Sir Robert's respect in the end. It was a hard time,

14   The siege of Rouen, showing many different ways of attacking a town.

however, when every move was suspected as the beginnings of violence: Carey even called his council together and ordered his troops out when he heard the borderers were planning a football match!

When his father died, Robert Carey continued to act as warden but he badgered Burghley, Elizabeth's chief minister, who disliked him considerably, to get him his patent of office and his pay. Nothing happened for a year, so Carey decided to go to Court, even though he had not been called. There he was warned by everyone that the Queen would be furious with him. No one would announce him at first, but after a while he got an old friend to go to

15   Nonsuch Palace, one of the prettiest royal palaces of the Elizabethan age.

Elizabeth to say that he had not seen her for a year and could no longer contain himself — he simply had to see her. The Queen enjoyed flattery and called him in. Later, she went to shoot deer leaning on his arm, to the amazement of those who had forecast his absolute fall from favour. What was more to the point, she gave him his patent and £500 back pay.

However, in the confusion that was quite typical of Elizabethan appointments, Carey was supplanted as warden by Lord Willoughby, and was soon back at Court anxious for a new appointment. He was offered the wardenship of the Middle March, which had been ruled by a weak and feckless warden for many years and was very much run down. Carey accepted and was soon back at work hanging thieves and chasing outlaws.   His opponents thought that his ardour would soon cool and sent him a rude message saying that he was 'like the first

puff of a haggis, hottest at first'. But they soon learned that he could keep the heat up for a long time.

In March 1603, Carey returned to Court to find the Queen lying on cushions in her inner lodgings, and looking very ill. She sighed a great deal, but seemed pleased to see him. For a long while she would not go to bed or take food or medicine. Carey realized she was dying and so he wrote to his old friend James I to warn him and to say that he would be the first to bring him the news of Elizabeth's death. He watched closely at Court, but the Queen's Council was watching him, and at her death tried to stop him rushing off to Scotland.

Carey escaped, however, and completed the journey in three days, despite a fall during which his horse kicked him badly on the head. James said he would treat him well when he came to England as a reward for bringing him the news of his accession, but he soon forgot his promises and the Careys had to make do with second best. Yet Robert's luck held. There was one

16   Queen Elizabeth I in later life.

post no one seemed to want, that of nurse and guardian to the four-year-old Duke of York. He was weak and ailing, could not yet walk, indeed he could barely stand, and was not yet able to talk. He was the King's second son, and clearly would die soon, so nobody minded the Careys looking after him. Lady Carey cared for him very well, protecting him from his father's rough inclinations to cut the string of his tongue to make him talk and put him in iron boots to make him walk. Under her gentle care, he grew sturdy and strong, and when his elder brother died in 1612 he became Prince of Wales and Sir Robert Carey became his Chamberlain.

17   **Charles I as a young man.**

18   *bottom right* **Robert Carey, Earl of Monmouth.**

The Prince of Wales eventually became Charles I and Carey was made Earl of Monmouth. His financial problems now resolved and his children well married, he spent his last years writing the memoirs from which this account is taken. He died in 1639.

5 THE ADVENTURER:
Sir Thomas Stucley

Lord Burghley called him a rakehell, and many people called him worse, with full justice — cheat, pirate, traitor, almost any villainous name would apply. Yet he had such charm that he won his way through wherever he was. Thomas Stucley was born about 1525, near Ilfracombe in the West Country, the third of six children in a moderately wealthy and well-connected family. He could call many of the leading men of Devon cousin, and they all stuck by one another. They had to, for most of them were or had been pirates.

Throughout his life Stucley hinted to all who might listen that his father in Devon was not his real father, but that he was the illegitimate son of no less a person than King Henry VIII. There is no way of knowing for sure, and it seems most unlikely, but Stucley did talk on even terms with kings and queens to the day of his death, and they never suggested that he had no right to be so free with them.

Stucley became a soldier, attaching himself first to the household of Charles Brandon, Duke of Suffolk. He fought at Boulogne and on the Scottish border, and it was not long before he became a standard-bearer. When Brandon died, Stucley attached himself to another brother-in-law of Henry VIII, the Earl of Hertford, uncle to young Prince Edward. When Henry died and Edward became king, the Earl became Protector of the Realm and was created Duke of Somerset. Stucley was rising fast.

Unfortunately, Somerset had a rival, the Duke of Northumberland, who managed to force him from power. Stucley plotted with a Spanish friend, Julian Romero (whom we shall meet again) to restore Somerset, but he failed and in October 1551 was forced to flee to France. There he made firm friends at Court and was soon

19 **Charles Brandon, Duke of Suffolk, was brother-in-law to Henry VIII and Stucley's first master. Brandon lived from 1483 to 1545.**

fighting for France and learning more of the craft of war. However, he did not intend to stay there for ever, and he soon put into action his first really great plot.

In August 1552, he came home to England and went straight to Court, holding off arrest by showing a letter from the King of France recommending him in the warmest terms; the letter might have been about a brother sovereign. As soon as he could get a private word with those in authority, he began to tell an amazing story: he was really a double agent, and he would now reveal the plans the King of France was making for the invasion of England. King Edward's councillors didn't know what to believe, so they checked Stucley's story with the English ambassador to France and with the King of France himself. Naturally, the King said it was a pack of lies, so the Council put Stucley into the Tower of London, and at the same time checked the defences. The plot had failed.

20   This is another brother-in-law to King Henry VIII. He is Edward Seymour, Duke of Somerset, whom Stucley served after Brandon's death.

21   The Tower of London, where Stucley was imprisoned in Edward VI's reign.

In 1553 Edward died, and when Mary came to the throne Stucley was released. He went off to Brussels, carrying another warm, recommendatory letter, this time from the Queen of England. He fought against the French now, in the army of the Duke of Savoy, and did very well, but not well enough for his liking. He wanted to come home, but dared not, for he knew he would be arrested for debt. In October 1554, he wrote explaining his plight to Queen Mary, and she graciously gave him six months security from arrest.

Six months was enough, and he soon made a runaway marriage with the grand-daughter of one of London's richest alder-men, Thomas Curtis. What Curtis thought about the match we do not know, but Stucley spent his time in piracy or fighting for a while, so he cannot have been too much trouble to his father-in-law. But when Curtis died, Stucley was ready to pounce and he took over the whole estate for his own use. For a year and a half he lived like a prince in London, spending, it was said, £100 a day.

The money would not last for ever, and now there was a new Queen on the throne. Elizabeth was one of the few people who did not fall for Stucley's charm, perhaps because her sister had liked him so well. However, Robert Dudley, Elizabeth's favourite and, some said, her lover, was an old friend of Stucley's and spoke for him at the right moment. For Stucley had a new plot.

A French explorer had turned up in London trying to get backing for an expedition to colonize Florida, in America. Stucley liked the idea and was soon beating up support for an expedition with himself in charge. He had a couple of ships of his own and he persuaded some London merchants to lend him two more. He got weapons from the Royal Armoury and victuals from the Royal Provisions (though Elizabeth had sworn not to give him a penny), and with his last few pounds he gave

a magnificent party before setting off.

He did not get very far — with a fleet of ships and plenty of weapons the temptations were too strong; instead of going to America he hung around the Channel and the North Atlantic and pounced on foreign merchant-men. He landed his pirated goods in Ireland, where he had good friends, especially the powerful Shane O'Neill, who he had enter-tained in his London house on Thomas Curtis's money.

The complaints flowed in from all sides, not least from those who had put up money for the Florida venture; so Stucley was brought home to answer a charge of piracy. Amazingly, he got off — perhaps the Queen had had a certain return from Stucley's privateering, and felt that her investment had been sound. She noted, however, that he was not to be trusted, and this was the last time she would let him off.

22　A map of Ulster.

32

In 1565, Stucley decided to return to Ireland and make his way there. He had high ambitions of being made Knight Marshal under Lord Deputy Sidney. He planned to make himself lord of the land bordering on Shane O'Neill's territory in Ulster, where he too might rule like a prince.

His dream was rudely shattered by Elizabeth, who would not allow it. Stucley was undoubtedly furious, but he was soon plotting instead to be seneschal of Wexford and to build up his estate there. Once again he was deposed and his successor accused him of gross irregularities. Stucley was never one to go by the law book, so in 1569 he was in gaol, and his son Will was taken to England as a hostage.

Living in Ireland, surrounded by Catholic lords who resented English rule, Stucley could not help but be influenced. He now hated Elizabeth, and so longed to be a kind of prince of Ireland that he took on the views and religion of his neighbours. Like them he now looked to Philip of Spain for help. When he was freed from prison he managed to get his ten-year-old son returned to him from England and a ship of his own. He sailed, everyone thought, for England, but he landed in Spain.

At once, Stucley began to urge the King of Spain to invade England through Ireland, and he readily gave all the information about shipping, defences and harbours that an invading fleet would need. The King was interested, but very cautious by nature, so he gave Stucley a rich pension whilst he though the whole matter over.

Thomas hated all this waiting, for he was quite confident of success. 'I will eat my Christmas pie with the Lord Deputy', he boasted, and went on to say that he would pluck the George, the badge of the English order of chivalry, from his neck and replace it with the Spanish Order of the Golden Fleece. Philip was not so sure, but was gracious to Stucley, whom he knighted. Thomas was grateful in his turn, but felt this was no replacement for what he really wanted — to be Archduke of Ireland. So he went off with Philip's brother, Don Juan of Austria, to fight the Turks at Lepanto. It was a famous victory and Stucley, who had been in command of three galleys, covered himself with honour, so that when he arrived in Rome he was the hero of the hour. Princes and cardinals became his close friends, and the Pope listened eagerly as he bragged about ideas of sailing up the Thames and setting fire to Elizabeth's fleet.

Elizabeth meanwhile was furious that a subject of hers could talk like this and be supported by a king who had once desired to marry her. Stucley had received about £100,000 from Philip of Spain, and Elizabeth insisted as part of the treaty of 1575 that he and his like should get no more support. So it was now up to the Pope, and possibly Don Juan. Stucley plotted to marry Don Juan to Mary Stuart, and both

showed great interest, as well as the Pope. The invading force was to land at Liverpool, free Mary, and then take over England. Of course, Thomas Stucley would get his reward — the long-dreamt-of archduchy of Ireland. The leader of the enterprise would be Stucley's old friend Julian Romero. Stucley went north to join Don Juan in the Netherlands, but a sudden desperate crisis there made it impossible for Don Juan to join any expedition to England. It was all off.

25   Don Juan of Austria, an adventurer who was not adventurous enough for Stucley. He was a son of Emperor Charles V and became Governor of the Netherlands.

The rebels in the Low Countries had saved England from invasion.

Stucley miserably went back to Rome. His life was not safe; there were English assassins after him and he constantly wore a mail shirt under his clothes. On the way to Rome he heard that the nephew of Queen Elizabeth's chief minister was close at hand and he plotted to kidnap him, but he missed him — nothing seemed to work.

Then back in Rome in 1578, after all his years of pleading, he was given a galleon and 600 men. The galleon leaked badly and the men were mutinous, but at long last he was off to invade Ireland! No-one from the Irish community in Rome wanted to go,

but Stucley was not to be put off and he promptly shanghaied a number of them, including a bishop — always useful to have a bishop on a holy venture like a crusade, even an unwilling one.

They laboured across the Mediterranean, facing dreadful storms, mutinies, threats from Turks and pirates. Stucley knew he must put into port to refit before he could make Ireland and he decided on Lisbon, despite urgent warnings that he was not welcome there. On reaching Lisbon he had 4 metres (12 feet) of water in the hold and the ship needed urgent repairs. Stucley would have no truck with ordinary folk — he immediately demanded an interview with the King of Portugal, and naturally he got it.

The King was in the final stages of planning a crusade against the Moors. He dreamed he was like some medieval king and his nobles dreamed too — no one had

any practical sense. They certainly did not want to be involved in some crazy venture against England, with whom Portugal had had good relations for many years. The King urged Stucley to forget Ireland and join him in his crusade. The ship was quietly towed to the breakers' yard and the men put on shore. Stucley was interested. It was like the old Florida venture over again, and these mad Portuguese certainly needed the old captain's advice.

There was, however, a terrific squabble over the weapons. Stucley argued (correctly) that they were the Pope's, as he had paid for them, so that he (Stucley) had no right to loan them or to give them to the King of Portugal. Now he could, of course, sell them and 'bank' the money for the Pope. But the King had no spare money to line Stucley's pockets and so he impounded the armoury. Stucley was furious, but could do

26 Lisbon harbour in 1594, not long after Stucley
set sail from there for his last voyage.

nothing. When they all sailed off for Africa
he was still angry, but he was also worried,
for no one was taking his advice and there

was no doubt that these people badly
needed it

A battle was prepared, with Stucley in
command of the Italian troops. At Alcazar,
on 4 August 1578, the King of Portugal and
many of his men were slaughtered; amongst
them was Sir Thomas Stucley, Marquess of
Wexford. His last plot had failed.

6 THE CHURCHMAN:
Miles Coverdale

The change which took place in religion in Tudor times was the most violent and disturbing upset of the period. Because it was a time of great extremes in belief, the change was never constantly in one direction but veered from one extreme to the other and back again. The Roman Catholics, whilst prepared to recognize the need for reform in religion, were determined to hold on to their basic beliefs at whatever cost, attaching themselves firmly to the Pope and obedience to the Church's rulings. The Protestants wanted to get rid of all the ceremonial of the Roman faith, and what they saw as the magical element in it (whereby the Roman Catholics believed that the bread and wine consecrated in the mass really turned into God's body and blood).

The Protestants believed that every man — through study of the Bible and belief in God — could find a direct road to God, without the medium of the priest. In the middle of these two parties were those who wished to have an easy and gentle change that brought the best of both worlds. Naturally, they argued and fought with one another, and in this rough age they were quite willing to use harsh weapons. Many people on all sides died for their faith, because their enemies would not let them live with it and they refused to give it up.

A man who saw many of these frightening changes was Miles Coverdale. He was born in York in about 1488, right at the start of the Tudor age. Like many scholarly people, he went into a religious order to receive his education and became an Augustinian friar at Cambridge. There he learned much that was new, but set in a firmly Roman Catholic context. When he was made a priest in 1514, he was probably as good a Catholic as any other. The change in his life came in about 1520 when a new prior was appointed, named Robert Barnes.

Barnes was a great scholar, just back from studying abroad, where he had picked up many new ideas. He urged all the scholars in his house to study the great classic works of Roman literature to improve their knowledge and style of Latin, and he pressed them to look again at the Bible, especially the works of St Paul. They approached the Bible in a new way. In the past, people had rarely read it for what it contained, but had rather studied it in the way schoolchildren study a set book, using a lot of guides and interpretations. Barnes got his friars to read it afresh, as if it were a new book, to see what message it had for them. They did not study what the Church *said* the Bible meant, but the Bible itself, and for many of them there were a lot of surprises. The Church of their times did not seem to measure up with the ideals of the Church that St Paul was trying to build.

Barnes's teachings soon got him into trouble, for he preached in public against some of the things the Church was doing,

27 Coverdale's patron, Thomas Cromwell, at the height of his power. He looks quite a harsh man of business here, but Coverdale saw another side to his character. Thomas Cromwell lived from 1485 to 1540.

and he was taken to London to be tried as a heretic in 1526. Coverdale went with him to help with the defence, and there he met Thomas Cromwell (one day to be the King's chief minister), with whom he made friends. Coverdale was very distressed at what was being done to people like Barnes, and he thought of going abroad to a place where it would be safer to work, to join William Tyndale who was busy translating the Bible into English for all to read. But he must have felt that this would be cowardly and he decided instead to leave the Augustinian friars and go into Essex as a secret missionary to preach the new Gospel. He managed to keep going for a couple of years, but then when it became too dangerous he finally left for Hamburg to join Tyndale.

In Hamburg and in Antwerp, Coverdale assisted Tyndale in his translation of the Bible, keeping himself by correcting proof pages for printers for a small fee. In 1534, he set to work on his own translation of the Bible, which he completed in one year. By now his friend Cromwell was in power in England and it was safe to go back to London to help in the project of getting the first official translation of the Bible printed. He first went to Paris to try to get the job done but there the Inquisition, the Roman Catholic police, stopped the work and Coverdale was nearly caught. So

28 William Tyndale (1492-1536) made the first translation of the Bible into English.

29 *opposite* The title page of Coverdale's Bible, 1535. It was dedicated to Henry VIII. Most of the pictures are Biblical scenes, but at the bottom the King is shown giving a Bible to his bishops and nobles.

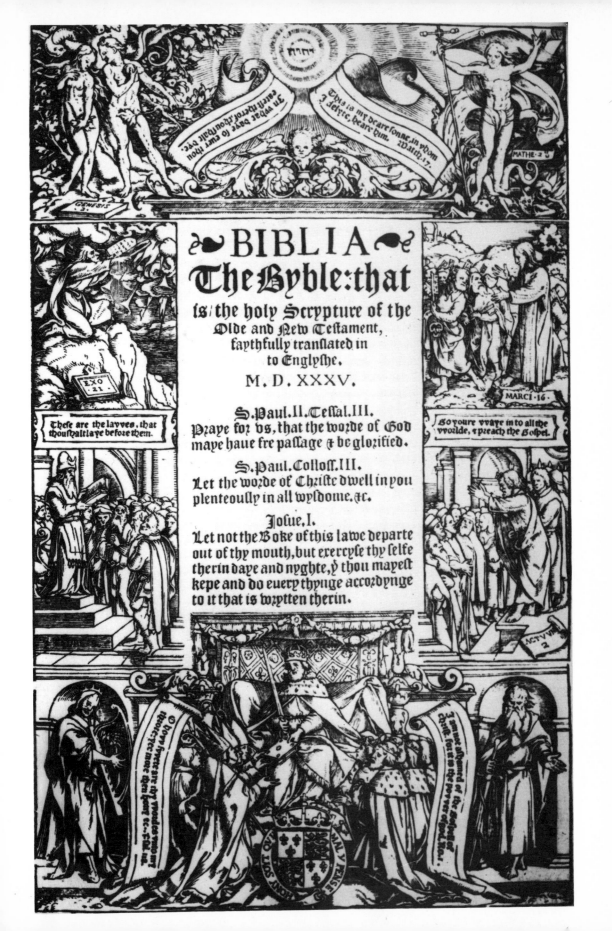

✦ BIBLIA ✦

The Byble:that

is/ the holy Scrypture of the
Olde and New Testament,
faythfully translated in
to Englyshe.

M. D. XXXV.

S. Paul. II. Tessal. III.
Praye for vs, that the worde of God
maye haue fre passage & be glorified.

S. Paul. Colloss. III.
Let the worde of Christe dwell in you
plenteously in all wysdome. &c.

Josue. I.
Let not the Boke of this lawe departe
out of thy mouth, but exercyse thy selfe
therin daye and nyghte, ý thou mayest
kepe and do euery thynge accordynge
to it that is wrytten therin.

This is my deare sonne, in whom I delyte, heare him. Math. 17.

These are the lawes, that thou shalt laye before them.

Go youre waye in to all the worlde, & preach the Gospel.

he returned to London, where the Bible was finally printed. Back in England, Coverdale helped Cromwell by travelling the country looking for those who were still following such Roman Catholic practices as worshipping saints like Thomas Becket. Perhaps there was a difference, but one cannot help but think that he was behaving just as the Inquisition had in Paris.

All went well for a while and like many Protestants Coverdale got married, just to show that it was reasonable for priests to marry, even though the Roman Catholic Church said it was wrong. He married a Scotswoman, Elizabeth Murchieson, who had escaped to England with her sister Agnes to avoid being prosecuted as a heretic at home. Agnes married another exile from

30 Queen Elizabeth I wrote this in her copy of Coverdale's Bible. Notice her signature.

Scotland, John Macalpine, and Coverdale was to find his brother-in-law very useful at a later stage.

Meanwhile the King was getting very worried about the direction in which Cromwell was taking the country, and he was particularly worried about the extreme Protestantism of the Church. He decided to backpedal, and did so with vigour. Cromwell was executed and Robert Barnes was burnt to death. Coverdale and Macalpine left for Germany, where Protestant rulers would assure their safety.

Macalpine went eventually to Denmark, where its King made him Professor of Religious Studies at the university, whilst Coverdale stayed in Strasbourg, meeting there one of the greatest of the Protestant reformers, John Calvin. He took his final degree of Doctor of Divinity at a local university, and went to Copenhagen to visit his relations for a while. Then in 1543 he was offered the post of assistant minister and schoolmaster at Bergzabern, about 40 miles north of Strasbourg. He spoke fluent German and enjoyed teaching, so he was happy there.

When Henry VIII died, his young son Edward came to the throne and the Protestants came back into favour once more; but Coverdale was not in a hurry to get back and wisely waited for an invitation to return, which came in March 1548. He began preaching at once and was most successful, being appointed a royal preacher. He was kept very busy on all the commissions set up to reform the Church, and was also engaged in the trials of some extreme Protestant heretics. For even the Protestants were willing to burn fellow Protestants to death if their views did not fit in. A German doctor called George van Parris was in England and Coverdale had to attend his trial as an interpreter for the poor man, who could speak little English, and so, one would have thought, was little risk as a converter of Englishmen to his views.

George, however, was burnt at the stake.

In June 1549, the people of the West Country rose in rebellion against the changes in religion. They wanted the old Roman Catholic service back again. Lord Russell was sent to quell the rebels and Coverdale went to preach to them. He was now over 60, but he showed great vigour and stayed on after the rebellion, preaching the new Gospel. The Bishop of Exeter at that time, Veysey, was 86 and in retirement in Worcestershire. He was a staunch Catholic and people soon began to compare Coverdale and Veysey. In 1551, Veysey was put out of the bishopric and Coverdale was elevated in his place. He tried hard to convert the people to Protestantism, but with little success; so great was the opposition that two attempts were made to poison him.

Coverdale had little time to make an impact, for in 1553 Mary came to the throne determined to turn the country back into a thoroughly Roman Catholic land. Coverdale was dismissed from his bishopric and old Bishop Veysey was put back in his place. Coverdale was told to keep to his house in London, though others were put straight into prison for their faith. Coverdale was brave enough to sign the declaration of faith that the imprisoned Protestants put out in May 1554 and tried to help fellow Protestants wherever possible.

Meanwhile, his brother-in-law in Denmark was agitating in his favour and the King of Denmark wrote three letters to Queen Mary begging for Coverdale's release. Eventually she agreed, and in February 1555 he sailed to Denmark. He did not stay there long, and soon joined a group of English Protestant exiles at Wesel. Later, he was invited back to

31 **Latimer preaching in London to Edward VI.**

his old ministry of Bergzabern. In 1557, he moved to join the English exiles at Aarau, and there it was noted that he had two children — we know no more of them than that. In 1558, he went to Geneva where Protestant scholars were hard at work on a new translation of the Bible.

Eventually, things changed in England, for on Mary's death in 1558, Queen Elizabeth came to the throne and brought back a mild form of Protestantism. Coverdale was in no hurry to return home, for he was now old and fat and found travel difficult. He returned in August 1559 and stayed with the Duchess of Suffolk, one of the leaders of the more extreme Protestants. He acted as schoolmaster to the children in her house, and he did a little preaching, but he would not accept his bishopric again. Whilst abroad he had become much more radical in his thinking, and he now joined those who objected most strongly to clergy wearing elaborate vestments, because it seemed to make them like the Roman Catholic priests.

Many people tried to get Coverdale to accept an appointment in the Church of England, for he was one of the founding fathers of the Church, who had worked hard for it and suffered and was now old and in want. He referred to himself in letters as 'poor old Miles'. He was eventually persuaded to become vicar of St Magnus by London Bridge, but two years later he resigned because he would not keep the order to wear vestments.

Coverdale survived the plague of 1563 and continued to preach. And when his wife died in 1565, he married again within a few months. In the last year of his life, he set up house in London with his new wife. He must have been a very resilient old man, but he died in January 1569, at the age of 81. He had seen violent changes, and there were more to come. He had stuck firm by his belief, and travelled far, making many friends. All found him humble, generous and kind, but like most of the

32   Bishop's vestments, which Coverdale did not wish to wear.

religious leaders of his day he had been a persecutor, too. Religion then was not about love, as we now see it, but about salvation, and who had the right way to God. If a man really believed he had the right way, then those who believed otherwise must be wrong, must be dangerous, and so they felt justified in killing them.

33   Miles Coverdale, Bishop of Exeter.

7 THE SOLDIER:
William, Lord Grey of Wilton

William succeeded to the family title — Lord Grey — in 1529, when he was 20 or 21 years of age. He soon decided that he would make his career as a soldier, and in the following year he took over the guardianship of the small castle of Hammes, a few miles from Calais. The English kings had been claiming the crown of France for nearly 200 years and some of them, particularly Edward III and Henry V, had won a lot of French territory. But others had lost much of it, and by the reign of Henry VIII the only land that remained under English control was the area round Calais. Henry was keen to expand this area and looked with great favour on men who had served him well there.

By 1544, Lord Grey had risen to the rank of colonel in the army, and at the siege of Montreuil he was shot through the shoulder. It was a lesson to him to wear armour, for at the time he was only wearing a leather jerkin and was armed with just a sword and a small shield. He was an impetuous man, and behaved as though he were living in the age before gunpowder. The next year, however, he was back with Henry's army besieging Boulogne, and he received his reward. He was moved from Hammes to the important post of governor of Guisnes,

34   **Men getting ready to fire a cannon. This picture appeared in a history of arms and war, published in 1535.**

a town with a strong castle and closer to Calais.

By the time Lord Grey got to Guisnes there was a truce in force and on both sides men were warned not to fight on pain of death. Grey observed, however, that the French were taking unfair advantage of the truce and were building a big rampart in a garden outside the town, to put their guns on when the truce finished. He wrote to the King to ask what he should do but the King, having agreed to the truce, could make only one formal reply — do nothing. Having written the letter with this instruction, the King called the messenger aside for a private word that actually he would be delighted if Lord Grey could throw down the rampart, but he could not publicly agree to it. The messenger returned with the letter which Lord Grey read to his council; then the messenger divulged the verbal instruction from the King. All of Grey's councillors said it was safer to follow the written instruction, but Grey decided to ignore their advice. Instead, he got the messenger to repeat the message so that his secretary could write it down, and then urged all his councillors to witness with their signatures that the King's message had been given to them reliably in these words.

That very night Lord Grey took a troop of men out quietly and they threw down the ramparts without the French hearing them. The following morning the messenger was despatched back to Court. When the King saw him he thought that Grey had sent him to confirm his instructions and muttered angrily, 'What, will he do it or no?' Naturally, when he heard that the job was done, and without any fighting, he was delighted. Lord Grey was in the King's good books.

In 1547, Lord Grey went as a senior commander with the Earl of Hertford's army into Scotland, where he fought with great distinction and set up modern fortifications. However, he was still as hot-headed as ever, and his commander-in-chief had to keep him from chasing the Scots, who came on in sudden sallies to attack the line of march of Lord Grey's troops. At times, though, nothing could restrain his instinct to charge, even when on one occasion he suffered a nasty wound from a pike that was thrust into his face and pinned his tongue to the roof of his mouth.

At the capture of Haddington, Lord Grey was faced with a very difficult problem, which he solved in a typical way. He was besieging a local fort where the defenders showed great courage and he was prepared to let them all go when he had captured it. All, that is, except one, who had shouted from the walls some foul abuse against the King of England. Grey would not want him to go free, but he was unable to identify him when the defenders came out. All the evidence pointed to a man called Newton, but when he was interrogated he claimed that it had not been him, but a man called Hamilton. So Grey ordered that they should fight each other to prove by God's judgement who was the man, the winner to go free. Newton was desperate because he knew that the evidence was strong against him and he managed to kill Hamilton. All around said it was unfair, and were for executing Newton; but Lord Grey kept the rules that he had made, and gave Newton his own robe and the gold chain he wore round his neck.

When the Earl of Hertford, now Duke of Somerset and ruler of all England as Lord Protector, returned to London, he left Grey in charge in the North, ruling the East March from Berwick — as Robert Carey (see p. 26) was to do at a later date. It was a costly business, because when Grey lost a battle it was his own men, mounted on his own horses and armed with his own armour, that were lost. In 1549, he came south and played a large part in quelling the risings against King Edward in Oxfordshire, Buckinghamshire and the West of England.

35 A town under siege. The people are being asked to surrender by the attackers. They look as though they are going to give in.

Lord Grey deserved favour, but he had allied himself with the wrong side and, when the Duke of Somerset fell from power in 1551, Lord Grey accompanied him to the Tower of London. However, he was too useful a man to be kept long in prison and Somerset's successor, the Duke of Northumberland, soon released him and sent him back to France to look after the castle and town of Guisnes.

For a while, all went well. Even though Lord Grey had been a close supporter of Northumberland in his bid to stop Mary coming to the throne on Edward's death, he was kept in his post after Mary's victory. It was to prove a hard position under Queen Mary. The governors of Calais and all the castles in the area kept warning her that the French were planning an attack and asked for help from her husband, King Philip of Spain. Early in January 1558, the attack came and Calais, which had taken Edward III a year to win, was lost to the French in a few days.

Now the pressure was all on Guisnes, where the French army arrived on 13 January. The town had no real walls and was easily overcome, the inhabitants withdrawing to the castle. That night, when the French were settled in the town, Grey had

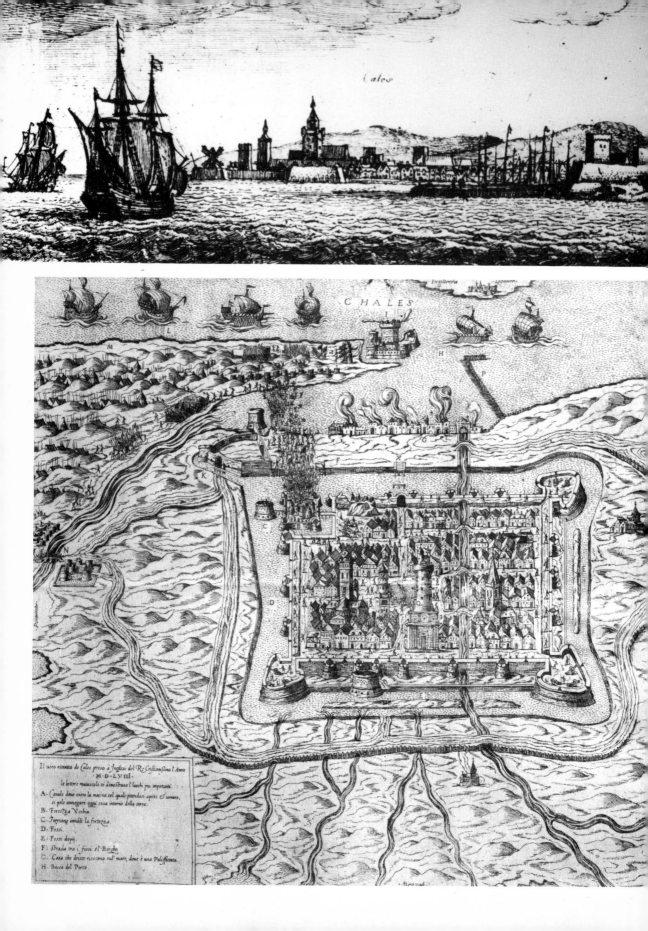

Cales

CHALES

Inghilterra Douer

Il uero ritratto de Cales preso à Inglesi del Re Cristianissimo l'Anno
M·D·LVIII·
le lettere maiuscole si dimostrano i luochi piu importanti

A. Canale doue entra la marea col quale potendosi aprire s'ascosa,
   si può annegare ogni cosa intorno della terra.
B. Fortezza Vechia.
C. Terreno innasi la fortezza.
D. Fossi.
E. Fossi doppi.
F. Strada tra i fossi e'l Borgo.
G. Casa che dietro cicisono sul mare, doue è una Palisficata.
H. Bocca del Porto.

his men burn it down — he would give the French no shelter. He had quite a good stock of gunpowder and his men steadily shot at the French whilst they laboured to dig trenches. By Monday, 17 January, the French had built trenches and emplacements for their heavy guns, and they began to play a concentrated fire on one weak part of the defences of the castle.

By about two o'clock they had made a sufficient breach to mount an attack; they easily ran up to the castle, loosing off a volley from their pistols and receiving from the English defenders 'a few pushes of the pike', as Lord Grey's son Arthur, who was present at the siege, recalled. They then retired to tell the rest of the army how easily they had made it to the defences, and so the

36   A view of Calais from the sea.

37   An aerial view of Calais. It looks a strong enough place. Why was so strong a fort captured?

38   Queen Mary and King Philip.

39 **The Duke of Guise, drawn a few years after capturing Calais.**

next wave came on more eagerly. 'Then a little more earnestly we leaned to our tackling, our cross-fire guns walked, our pikes and our guns, our pots of wild-fire were thrown at them, and our hand-guns hailed them, so that jolly Mr Gascony was sent down with more haste than he came up with good speed.'

That night the English worked hard to rebuild the defences which the cannon had shot down in the day, and they dug trenches to fight from. Lord Grey visited his soldiers in the breach to encourage them and found them in good heart, even though they had lost about 50 men and two officers.

On Tuesday morning, the French began a cannonade once more. After a while, they sent forward some Swiss observers to try to

40 **These mortars, designed to lob cannon-balls high in the air, are on movable carriages.**

check what damages their fire had done, but Lord Grey had given special orders that observers were to be driven off at all costs, so soon the Swiss were running for their lives. The cannons started once more, and Arthur Grey comments that the English were driven into their trenches to live like moles. The French had sent over some 9,000 cannon-balls in the two days of their attack.

On Wednesday, the battery broke out again at dawn and continued until ten o'clock, doing dreadful damage. While Lord Grey and his colleagues sat on a bench above the breach, one cannon-ball fell right in the middle of the bench and cut it in two. At about one o'clock the English saw that the leading French trenches were 'stuffed with regiments', so Lord Grey ordered all the men to stand their ground while he sent his sharpshooters to the top of the one remaining tower of the castle. He also got his gunnery officers to prepare their last remaining pots of wild-fire.

Then the attack came:

They approached the top of our trench, the pike is offered, to hardy blows it comes; then the Swiss come with a stately leisured step into the breach, and march up close together; the fight warms, the breach is all covered with our enemy. The fire from the tower now began, and not a bullet went astray. On the other side a detachment of our Spanish allies revealed themselves from their concealment and joined strongly in the battle, with heavy fighting on all sides.

After about an hour, the French withdrew and trained their cannon on the tower. It came down in two rounds of shot, killing many in that area, and the attack was pressed again. The English now had only a few guns for crossfire and so had to rely mainly on their pikes. They were desperately tired, but they fought viciously and as night came the French withdrew from the desperate struggle.

That night, Grey came down among the men once more, to see how much powder and shot were left and to encourage them. He ordered the dead to be buried, but as he pushed through the men huddled in the breach an unscabbarded sword pierced his foot and he had to retire to have the wound dressed. The English soldiers could hear that the French were at work and they lit torches to try to spy on them. The French were tying planks to barrels to make bridges for the final assault.

On Thursday, the cannons opened up once more and battered the English until three o'clock. Grey consulted with the commander of the Spanish detachment that King Philip had sent to help them, but the only solution they could offer was to set bombs in the way of the advancing French. Grey was so upset at the defeat he now faced that he leapt upon the rampart to show himself to the oncoming French, so inviting death, but a soldier pulled him down by his scarf. They had little time, and soon they were scuttling back to their last defensive position inside the keep, with Grey himself holding the door as the last man scrambled through. They barricaded the door and then to their horror found that some English, including Thomas Churchyard the poet, had been left outside. Churchyard told later of how Grey made a hole in the wall for them to wriggle through, the French so hard on their tails that they had to turn round at once and shoot through the hole and push with their pikes whilst material was brought up to block it.

As night drew on, the Duke of Guise sent a trumpeter to call Lord Grey to a parley. The English soldiers were now quite sure that they faced defeat and flocked round their commander to beg him to accept terms. He quietly reproved them and sent them back to their posts. Before the parley could begin, hostages had to be exchanged; Arthur Grey was sent with the English hostages to the French camp and he later recalled that dark journey, treading first on English bodies, 'some of them still sprawling and groaning', and later — with grim satisfaction — on as many French carcasses.

Grey sent Thomas Churchyard to negotiate. He set off miserably, wading through the water which surrounded the castle, treading carefully for fear of caltrops, balls of iron with long iron spikes scattered around by the French to catch the unwary. He found the Duke of Guise sure of victory and none of the poet's brave boasting could move him from that position. The English were to give up the castle and march out without marks of honour — that is, without drums and trumpets playing and flags flying.

Churchyard gave this message to Lord Grey, but the brave commander was determined not to give in. Instead he spoke movingly to his men of honour and of how they should sell their skins dearly. But they replied that such a policy was cutting their own throats and if Grey did not give in they would throw him over the wall. So, finally, the agreement was made: the castle was to be given up with its contents undamaged, the men could march out with their weapons and possessions undisturbed, but with no drums, trumpets or flags, and the officers were to go into French captivity until they could be ransomed.

The following afternoon Lord Grey yielded the keys of the castle and the Duke of Guise promptly razed it to the ground, so that it should never again be used by foreign invaders of France. At home, Lord Grey was recognized for his bravery and was awarded a knighthood of the garter, but he had to stay as a prisoner in France until money could be raised to release him. The French allowed him home to attend the coronation of Queen Elizabeth in 1558, but then he had to return until one of his estates had been sold to make up the ransom money of 24,000 crowns (£6,000).

By 1560 Lord Grey was home and fighting again in Scotland, where he led an attack on Leith. He showed his usual reckless courage, but allowed himself to be pushed into a hasty and under-manned attack on heavy defences, which was easily repulsed. Everyone blamed everyone else, and Lord Grey felt increasingly put upon. He was now a comparatively old man and having always lived in the past, when knights were bold and daring rather than cool and calculating, he could never understand that courage was not everything.

Grey was made warden of the East March again, but died soon after his appointment in December 1562. His funeral was a splendid affair — everywhere was hung richly with black, touched with white satin crosses and finely painted and embroidered coats of arms. Many distinguished people attended the stately ceremony and the fine dinner that followed. It marked the end of an era.

41   **This is believed to be a portrait of Lord Grey in old age.**

50

8 THE MERCHANT ADVENTURER:

John Isham

The Ishams were living in Northamptonshire in the fourteenth century and have continued to live there right up to the present day. John's father was called Euseby Isham, and he bred a most distinguished family. First came Gyles, who was educated as a lawyer at the Middle Temple and became steward to the Earl of Bedford (father-in-law to Lady Hoby's mother-in-law, a distant but interesting connection). Gyles served as a Member of Parliament, and was good to his younger brothers, lending them money and using his influence with the important people he met on their behalf. The next oldest was Robert, who was sent to Christ's College in Cambridge and became a priest. He did well in the Church and was a royal chaplain to Queen Mary; but as a staunch Roman Catholic he did not do so well when Queen Elizabeth came to the throne.

The three younger brothers — Gregory, John (who was born in 1525) and Henry — were not given the fine education that Gyles and Robert had had. John's son said that his father went to school until he was 16, but the spelling in his account books would disgrace an infant: he often found it difficult to spell his own father's name. But spelling was not everything in those days and these three boys valued arithmetic much higher, for they were sent to the City of London to be made apprentices to merchants.

There had been Ishams operating in the City earlier in the century, and certainly this was a good time to become a merchant. Trade was booming and for the modest fee of some £5 a willing lad could be apprenticed to a merchant and quickly learn his trade. It was no doubt a rather daunting prospect for a country boy to come up to London and go to the grand Mercers' Hall, to be presented to the assembled wardens there and hear the rules — no dice playing or gambling, no one to wear beards, each apprentice to keep to his own master. On the other hand, it must have been exciting to join this rich and secure company within which so many fortunes were made.

Gregory went to London in 1537 and had completed his apprenticeship and been made a freeman of his company by 1546. This was the year in which old Euseby died, leaving precious little to his three younger sons — John got £3 6s 8d (£3.33) — so they all knew they had to work for a living. John was apprenticed in 1542, and Henry joined his brothers somewhat later. John recalled little from the time of his apprenticeship other than the tedious and tiresome job of carrying buckets of water from the River Thames to his master's house. Think of all the gallons they must have used, all to be carried on one sore pair of shoulders.

The three brothers were all concerned with the cloth trade between England and the great international port of Antwerp. Ships bearing goods from all over the known

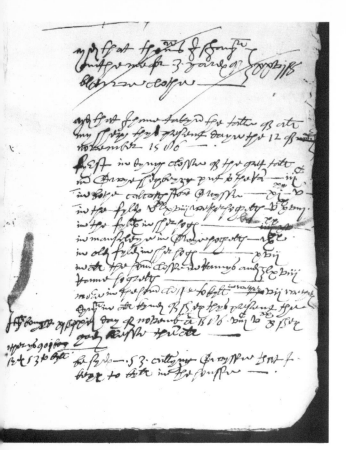

42 An extract from John Isham's account book. The transcript of part of this page is shown above right.

Memorandum that I have takyn the talle of all my shep thys present daye the 12 of november 1586

fyrst in dynges closse of the gret tall

in Ewye shep beyng put to the Ram	iii^c
in bothe calcattes store Ewysse	xi^{xx}v
in the fylds v^{xx} xviii wetherhogrells	v^{xx}xviii
in the fylds in sherhogs	iiii^{xx}xv
in manseleye in Ewye hogrells	ix^{xx}
in old fyld in sherhogs	xvii
in all the home closse in Ramys and) Rame hogrells)	lx viii

more in the home closse to kyll in wetheys   vii wetheys

Summa: in all kynd of shep thys present the xii day of november 1586 viii v^{xx} x shep god blesse them all

Item: bought xi shep so ther ys 901 besydes 53 to kyll

besydes — 53 culling Ewysse that I kepp to kyll in the housse

43 A procession passing the Mercers' Hall (far side of the road) in London.

world and beyond came into Antwerp — rough furs from farthest Russia, spices from the East, carpets from Persia and fine silks and satins from Italy. The Isham brothers learned this trade well; they sold woollen cloths from England in Antwerp and used the money to buy fine luxury

Rustica Anglicana   *Modus vendendi Lupos pisces apud Anglos*   *Paremptitius*

44   Market women at work and an apprentice getting water.

goods which they brought back to England and sold to courtiers and rich men.

However, this trade needed money, and as we have seen the Ishams could not rely

45   The Stock Exchange at Antwerp, where all the rich traders met, including the English.

on their father's wealth. John wisely married a rich widow and, as we shall see, this marriage, made originally for money, made a very happy family. In 1552, he married Elizabeth, widow of Leonard Barker, a mercer and merchant adventurer with much property and wealth. John at once had some capital to use and an estate to administer for gain. However, it was not all easy: one nasty and expensive job was cleaning

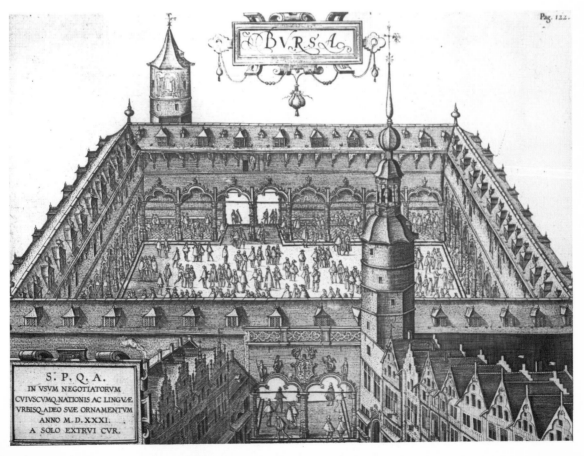

BVRSA

Pag. 122.

S. P. Q. A.
IN VSVM NEGOTIATORVM
CVIVSCVMQ. NATIONIS AC LINGVÆ
VRBISQ. ADEO SVÆ ORNAMENTVM
ANNO M. D. XXXI.
A SOLO EXTRVI CVR.

46 An Elizabethan merchant has just checked the loading of his ship and is coming back on shore.

out the lavatories of a row of houses in Bassinghall Street. Of course, John did not do it himself, but he must have been angry when he received the bill and found he had to pay £1 per house.

Another source of finance was his elder brother Gregory, who was soon doing very good business indeed. He too had married a rich heiress, and in the year following his freedom of the company his business turned over £1,500. By the time he died, he had invested about £8,000 in land. Although he left little ready cash and only a small store of silver and gold plate (ready to be pawned to raise cash at need), his warehouses in Antwerp and London were stuffed with goods. His houses in London and in the country were well furnished and richly hung with tapestries and paintings. He had a pair of virginals that would have gladdened the heart of Thomas Whythorne (see p. 57).

Gregory had made money fast, which he achieved by making his money work for him. He operated on credit a great deal of the time, finely calculating the point when he could most profitably pay his debts. Spare cash he loaned out to noblemen who needed ready money and were willing to pledge their land; if the money did not come back the land would be Gregory's at a very cheap price. So good was the business (even though there were harsh laws against lending money at interest) that Gregory would borrow money at a low interest just to lend it elsewhere at a high rate.

Gregory was kind to his younger brothers and let both John and Henry have easy loans. They worked together quite a lot, and Henry was certainly a very useful business partner after he had gained the office of controller of the customs of London. John and Henry took over many of Gregory's suppliers and customers after his death, and wound up his estate very creditably — they made nearly 100 per cent profit on the cloth in his warehouse. They also took on the duty of looking after Gregory's son, and did the job faithfully and well. When the boy went to the Middle Temple to learn law, they paid out £15 for his clothes, £13 for a furnished room for him and £5 in fees — schooling for the son of a rich merchant was a costly affair.

The business needed a great deal of energy and care. Isham had to ride out to make bargains with the producers of woollens in East Anglia, the West Country, Berkshire, and as far north as Halifax. To tempt people to let him have their wares at a good price, he would take fine things brought from Antwerp, and sometimes he carried out shopping requests. His imports often contained small parcels of various things, got in specially for a good supplier or customer.

John continued to use money well, as his brother had done. He often had spare cash in Antwerp, waiting from the sales of English wools until a cargo of Italian goods should arrive. He was not a man to

47   The cloth hall and wool market at Chipping Campden, Gloucestershire. Many London merchants rode in here to do business with the local farmers.

48   A Flemish weaver hard at work making a little money for his family, and some for the merchant.

let cash lie idle. He would find Englishmen going abroad who needed foreign money to draw on in Antwerp, and sell them a 'bill of exchange' — what we now would call a traveller's cheque — using the English money so gained to buy more goods or to loan at interest.

Although John seems a little like a miser at times, he was really very adventurous, because there was always great risk in his business. A customer might go bankrupt (a horrible thought), or a cargo of very expensive silks might get damaged, which so easily could happen to such a delicate material. Worst of all, the ships carrying John's cargoes could sink. John was always sure to divide up his cargoes between as many ships as he could in order to reduce the risk of heavy losses.. If you want to know what he felt like, you should read the opening scene in Shakespeare's play *The Merchant of Venice,* which is all about this subject.

The biggest danger for the Isham brothers,

however, came from the increasing discord between England and Spain, which led to the Spaniards closing the port of Antwerp to the English. This was a dreadful blow, and the traders had to take desperate measures — such as trying to move the market to Emden, Hamburg or Danzig. The danger signs were all out for merchants, but John Isham had long planned his escape route, for he was a canny man.

In 1560, with the help of his brother Robert the priest, John had purchased an estate in Northamptonshire called Lamport Manor. At first, this was just an investment. He had his fine house in London, bought that same year, with its many different rooms, including a counting house where he wrote up his accounts and a brushing room where bales of cloth were opened and prepared for sale. He also had a little place in the country at Tottenham (now part of North London) where he went with his family for weekends and which supplied him with fresh vegetables. When

49 Isham looks well satisfied with his fine clothes, his coat of arms and his expensive clock. His account books are included in the picture.

his son became sick, he sent him to Tottenham to recuperate.

Life continued well enough in London in the 1560s and in 1567 John was honoured by being made a warden of his company. He had set up memorials to Dick Whittington, an early mercer, and Dean Colet, who had started the school which the mercers patronized. He also gave a splendid dinner at the Mercers' Hall, and his son, who was only a boy at the time, recalled long afterwards the extraordinary sight of 33 carcasses of deer stored in the gallery of his father's house, waiting to be transported to the mercers' kitchen to feed the hungry diners on that occasion.

Even so, John Isham still carefully went on preparing his escape route, and in the following year began to build a fine house at Lamport. In 1572, he decided that trade had got so bad that he would retire and enjoy his Northamptonshire estate, leaving others to risk and adventure in the City. He became a JP, like Sir Nathaniel Bacon (see p. 7), and later was sheriff of the county. For a while in the late 1570s he seems to have returned to London and to business, but the episode did not last long. He was now a confirmed country gentleman.

John's son recorded a little about his father's personal life, from his own point of view. He remembered him as an easily angered, somewhat severe man to his children, but noted that when they left home to go to college he would turn aside his head to hide his tears, for he was at heart very affectionate. He had many friends, and never spared himself any trouble to help them. Nor was he a man to do an enemy down when he was in financial trouble. He was not a Shylock (see *The Merchant of Venice*), insisting on forfeits

being paid. Anyone whose business had declined and could not pay his debts would meet with kind treatment from John Isham. He was fond of a joke, despite his stern looks, and was for ever telling stories and repeating proverbs. He was a big, fat man who loved food and good company.

When John Isham lay on his deathbed, he called everyone to come and shake his hand, saying to them all, warmly and lovingly, 'Heart and hand both'. He was not long in pain, for shortly before his death he said to his manservant, 'Hark, how I wheeze', and then when they had turned him over to be more comfortable he held his eldest son's hand and said, 'Now heart and hand to God', and shortly after died. He had shaken hands on many a good bargain in his life and trusted to the old way of showing his faith.

9 THE MUSICIAN:
Thomas Whythorne

Thomas was probably born at Chard in Somerset in about 1528. His father owned some property, so their life was quite comfortable, but it was clear that his children would have to support themselves. Thomas went to school early in his life, where he began to learn reading, writing and singing, probably his first introduction to music. He must have shown some promise, for at the age of ten he was sent off to learn more from his uncle, a priest who lived some five miles out of Oxford. His uncle asked him what career would suit him: would he choose to be a priest, a doctor or a lawyer? As Thomas knew nothing of these things he though it best to say no to all of them, but when his uncle asked whether he would like to go on to learn some more grammar and music he was full of enthusiasm.

So Thomas's uncle packed him off to a famous school at Oxford, Magdalen College School, where Whythorne was a chorister for six years. It is interesting that his first contact with his family whilst at school came after he had been there two years, when his uncle wrote with news of himself and of Thomas's parents, and urging him to work hard. He obviously cherished that letter, for he remembered it well when he sat down to write his autobiography 36 years later.

After school, he went on to Magdalen College itself, but one year later his uncle died, leaving Thomas his furniture but little else, and so he had to leave college and go to London to make his fortune. He did not find it so hard, for throughout his life he loved London above all places. There he was lucky enough to find a place in the house of a well-known poet and musician called John Heywood. He remained with Heywood for three years, earning his keep by working as a servant to the poet (often copying out his verses in his best handwriting), and receiving tuition on how to play the lute and the virginals (roughly equivalent to our guitar and piano) and also how to write poetry.

When he felt he had learned enough to make his own way, he took a room in London and furnished it with what his uncle had left him. This room was 'home' to Whythorne for a good part of his life for, although he often took jobs that meant living in with another family, he always kept his room to go back to when he wanted to be on his own. He was very active in these days, learning to play even more instruments, learning to dance and to fence, and in general preparing himself for his life as a tutor to the wives and children of gentlemen. He became very interested in painting and spent some of his small store of cash on a large painting of the goddess of music and on having his own portrait done on the lid of his virginals case.

He now began his career as a tutor, and at once was plagued with something other

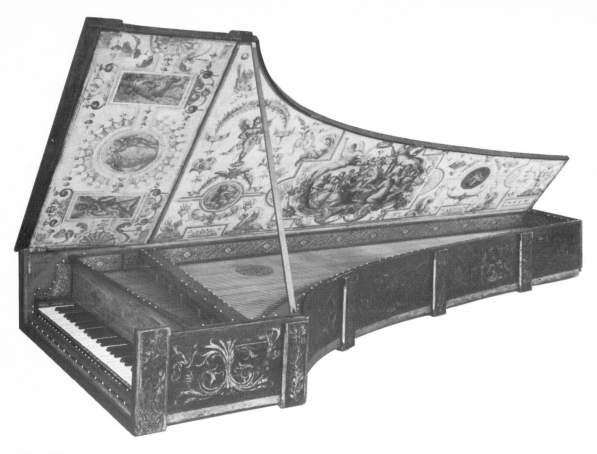

50   This virginal was made for Queen Elizabeth.
It is typical of the elaborate decorations on
Elizabethan musical instruments.

51   One of the many portraits Thomas Whythorne
had painted of himself. This one was commissioned
in 1569 when Thomas was 41. Notice the coat of
arms he had included.

people might have enjoyed: he was pursued
by women, or so he says in his autobiography. Wherever he went, women seemed
to fall for him, whilst he himself never
realized what was happening until too
late and then he was so bashful and shy he
could not respond. On his first appointment, a servant girl kept leaving love letters
between the stings of his lute. When his
employers found out, she was sacked. Next,
he accepted a post with a widow who
showered him with affection and bought
him clothes and rings. When he did not seem
to be very lovesome in return, she called
him 'huddypick' — a simple fool.

52 **Three musical ladies such as Thomas Whythorne might have taught. Notice that the music was written slightly differently then.**

Thomas enjoyed his new clothes, however, and invested in his second portrait. Since the last one was painted he had had a bout of ague, a dreadful disease rather like malaria in its effects, and he had aged in his appearance. He decided he would like to move in higher circles and planned to join the household of the Duke of Northumberland, protector of the Realm for the boy-king Edward VI, but the widow persuaded him to stay on with her. He would have lost both ways, for it was not long before the Duke lost his head in the plot to put his son and daughter-in-law, Lady Jane Grey, on the throne. But with the widow things went badly too, for she lost all her money, and Thomas, with some regrets, left her service.

Thomas then decided on a tour abroad, to learn languages and see the sights, and to study music as practised in other countries. He spent six months in the Netherlands, where he was shocked by the drunkenness of the people, and then went for a further six months to Italy, coming home through France. He had learned a lot and was hopeful of great success in London with a book he wrote about his travels. He also felt ready to marry.

The girl he picked on was ideal in most respects — beautiful, good-natured and wise — but she was the daughter of a substantial lawyer who plainly did not think much of a mere musician as a son-in-law. Thomas dressed up in fine clothes and attended on her like a courtier of the Queen, writing love songs to sing to her. But soon a rich suitor came along and swept her off her feet, and Thomas had to look elsewhere.

Meanwhile, he took a job in the house of Ambrose Dudley, a son of the Duke of Northumberland who had been executed. He was promised a fine reward — an annuity of nearly £7 a year — and the ladies of the household were as ever friendly. Thomas called them all by pet-names — Governor, Friend, Aunt, Sister, and the youngest of all he called Mother for a joke. But he did not stop there long, for Dudley lost all his money fighting for the Queen abroad and Whythorne could not afford to give his services free.

This time he moved to a family who lived out of London, and there got into a pickle over women, as usual. Close by there lived a rich old man who had a house-keeper called Elizabeth, an elderly lady who would certainly inherit all her master's money when he died. The servants in Why-thorne's household were often asked over to meals by Elizabeth, a generous and friendly lady, who soon had her eye on Thomas. She asked the family chaplain to bring him over one evening, and after rather too much to drink nearly persuaded Thomas that a marriage there and then was possible. The servants ribbed him a lot about this, and after a while began to tell him that Elizabeth had fallen ill for love of him and lay dying. He did not know what to believe, but eventually persuaded some girls to go over

53 **A musical party with a flute, dulcimer and lute.**

Crispin de Pas invent. excudit.

with him, believing that there was safety in numbers. He found Elizabeth was ill, but assured himself that love was not the cause and that she would recover.

He soon left that post and took another with a family who lived some five miles out of London. He now felt in a position to make conditions for his employment. He agreed to live in for the week only, taking weekends off in London, and to act only as tutor with no duties as a servant — his experience in the servants' hall in his last job had quite put him off.

The lady of the household had been at Court and talked interestingly of religious matters and how things went in the City. But her conversation rapidly veered towards descriptions of the love life of courtiers, and how the stars influenced people in love. Thomas carefully noted that she was becoming separated from her husband and prepared to be off, arranging another job with a family living three or four miles on the other side of London. However, his employer begged him not to leave her, saying that her daughter was about to marry and desperately needed Thomas's tuition to make her seem a fine, cultivated lady in her husband's eyes. Thomas relented and agreed to serve in both families, week and week about.

This left Thomas in a sad and sorry state, for he was now being pursued by both his employers' wives. Also his landlady in London, a widow with two children, was beginning to make eyes at him. The time had come to cut and run, so in 1559 he agreed to go to Cambridge University to help teach William Bromfield, son of a rich and important City gentleman.

Cambridge University was reserved for men in those days, so Thomas must have felt he would be safe there. Indeed, apart from a squabble with William's college tutor, he spent two happy years polishing up his knowledge of Italian and his skill in music, and reading a number of inter-esting books on religion. The college tutor proved a great nuisance at first: he did not see why young Bromfield needed an extra teacher from outside the university and persisted in snubbing Whythorne and treating him as though he were a student. In those days, students had to show great respect to their teachers, taking off their caps when they met them in the streets and 'giving them the wall' — that is, allowing the teacher to walk on the wall side of the pavement so as not to be splashed by mud from the dirty roads. Thomas kept his cap firmly on his head and took the wall himself. He was too old to be treated like a student, he thought.

When William left Cambridge University, Thomas returned with him to London, still in the employ of William's father (whose first name was also William). William the elder was away at war and wanted someone to look after his business for him, and no doubt keep a friendly eye on his son as well. It proved a difficult task. Thomas soon found that other merchants and officials were busy trying to do down Bromfield in his absence, and he knew he was neither strong enough nor sufficiently experienced to cope. Then Bromfield was wounded, and soon after died. Whythorne had to stay in London while an outbreak of plague was driving all those who could leave away into the country. Although he was terrified of getting the plague himself, Thomas stuck faithfully to the job he had been given.

In 1571 Whythorne decided to publish all the songs he had written. These were called madrigals. Each singer had a different part with different words to sing, rather like the way some people sing the part-song 'London's burning'. He had written both the words and the music and was justifiably proud of his work, setting as a frontispiece to his book a brand new portrait of himself with a coat of arms to show he was now a man of means.

54 **The portrait Thomas Whythorne commissioned as the frontispiece for one of his books.**

55 **A beautifully decorated Elizabethan harpsichord made in 1574.**

Thomas had not finished with women, though, and now he was approached by a marriage-broker, a person who made it his business to introduce couples (for a fee, of course) as marriage bureaux do today. The marriage-broker offered to introduce Thomas to a young widow with no children who had nearly £67 worth of property and £20 a year in income. Thomas was very keen on the match, but soon became disturbed by her strange behaviour. By what he says, it sounds as though the poor lady was mentally ill, so he had to withdraw from the match.

Thomas was now the Master of the Archbishop of Canterbury's Chapel, a very important post, which pleased him greatly. Perhaps it also did the trick with marriage too, for in 1577 he married a spinster, and we believe they lived happily. We know little of his career after 1576, when his autobiography was written, for he did not keep it up to date. In 1590, he published some more music — duets this time, a form new to England. He died in 1596.

10 THREE CRIMINALS:
Browne, Phillips and Fennor

The Tudors had to cope with a crime wave that seemed to them worse than any other in history. Wherever they turned, in towns especially but often in the country as well, they ran across what they called 'rogues and vagabonds'. These, like every group of criminals, contained a large number of juvenile delinquents. We do not know for sure why the problem was so bad. Perhaps the structure of the population had something to do with it. It certainly meant that

there were more young criminals, for there were more young people than old in Elizabeth's reign simply because people did not live as long then as we do now. It was probably also brought about by a movement of people away from the villages into the towns. At this time, much land was being enclosed to rear sheep, so fewer workers were needed in the countryside. Those who lost their jobs hoped to find work in the towns, but they rarely did. Another cause of the crime wave was the return of soldiers and sailors released from service after wars. They roamed around, often still with their weapons, looking for work but finding crime easier.

Our first criminal is called Ned Browne, whose life story was published by a writer who specialized in true crime stories. Perhaps he embroidered it a bit, as writers will, but it seems substantially true. Ned had good, honest parents who brought him up well and gave him a good education, but he was a deceitful boy from earliest youth and was soon engaged on a career of shoplifting. He got into bad company very quickly and learned the art of cutting purses. In Tudor times, people kept their

56   This is a forged passport with which a beggar travelled through England in 1596. An official in each county the beggar passed through signed it to state that he behaved well. The county names are on the left.

63

money in purses that hung from two strings attached to the belt. A man with a sharp knife in the palm of one hand would bump into a likely looking chap, draw the knife across the purse-strings, and the purse fell with a pleasant chink into his other hand, held ready below.

That was one way of making money, but Ned soon found others. He would see a rich lady with a purse at her belt and go up to her as if she were an old friend, put his arms round her and kiss her warmly. When she had escaped from this bear hug she would no doubt slap his face and he would apologise, say he had mistaken her for someone else and go away red-faced, but with the purse in his possession. In a crowd, a gentleman could have his money stolen by two cut-purses, one dropping a key or something in front of him and jostling him, and the other taking the purse. The gentleman would hotly accuse the man who had dropped the key, who would let himself be searched to prove that the gentleman was mistaken. Later, the thieves would share the booty — if the one could find the other, that is.

Ned got up to all sorts of tricks. He posed as an alchemist able to turn lead into gold, but needing money to build a laboratory — and some fool always put up the money in the hope of a rich return. He used the same disguise to sell love-potions of coloured water or deadly poisons to use on your enemies. At other times, Ned pretended to be a travel agent, offering to set up a wonderful trip abroad for a young gentleman but needing to have an advance of the money first, of course. Sometimes he disguised himself as a rich man and showed forged documents to prove that he was owed great sums of money that would shortly fall due. Pretending he needed ready cash in a hurry for a venture abroad, Ned would sell these documents at a reduced price to some poor fool who would then try to reclaim the money, only to find there was none due. Or, of course, he could simply play cards or dice, using his own specially doctored pack and loaded dice.

If the going got too hot, Ned could always slip across to France for a while, but he was such a master at disguise that he was very rarely known. He even possessed a false tail to disguise his horse. This horse once gave him a great adventure, which he boasted about till the day of his death. He was riding into Berkshire one day when he met a fat priest. Having been well educated, Ned could make himself acceptable to all types of company, high and low, and the priest quite took to him. Ned also took to the priest, for he saw that he carried a large sum of money in a cap-case attached firmly to his saddle. The priest, who said he was going to buy some land, admired Ned's

horse greatly and as they rode along they bargained for an exchange. Eventually, Ned agreed to accept the priest's horse and nearly £7 in cash in return for his own fine horse. When they stopped for a meal Ned made an excuse to go to the stable and there he tied a hair tightly round his horse's leg, using a special knot that he could quickly undo. After the meal they exchanged horses and rode on, but soon the priest's newly acquired horse began to limp. The priest grew angry and said Ned had given him a bad bargain, but Ned replied that the priest must be riding incorrectly and offered to ride her for a few minutes to see what the matter was. So once more they exchanged horses, but did not bother to change saddles. Ned bent down and felt the horse's leg, loosing the hair; then he mounted and rode off, the horse going perfectly. Ned rode faster and faster, and soon the priest's shouts grew softer and softer, until he could no longer hear them and quite forgot him! However, like so many of his friends, Ned ended up on the gallows.

It would be wrong to think that all Tudor criminals were men. In the 1590s, a woman called Judith Phillips, alias Doll Phillips, alias Doll Pope, was in the same line of business. She pretended to have magical powers, to know all that could be known, now and in the future, and many villains employed her. In 1595 her employer was a Mr Peters, who wanted to marry a wealthy widow and had chosen Mrs Mescall, a rich tripe-seller some 60 years of age who might be expected to die shortly after her marriage and leave the delighted Mr Peters her money, her jewels and her property. Unfortunately, Mrs Mescall had no wish to marry, so Doll was used to persuade her.

Peters primed Doll with a lot of information about the widow and Doll visited the old lady to 'read her palm'. With great mystification and much mumbo-jumbo, Doll took the widow's hand and began to

57 An ale house, the forerunner of our public houses.

spy in it all sorts of details about Mrs Mescall's private life. 'How know you that?', she kept saying, amazed at Doll's skill, whilst Doll cleverly avoided answering. When the widow was completely won over, she asked Doll to tell her the future. Doll agreed, but said that it could only be done in three days' time, and as proof of her honesty and wizardry she would perform a great marvel. She asked Mrs Mescall to gather together all the gold she had in the house, which the old lady eagerly did — some coins, a gold chain, seven rings and a whistle. Doll ceremoniously wrapped these up in a piece of cloth and then apparently handed the bundle back to the widow. In fact, she had switched them for a parcel of stones similarly wrapped which she had thoughtfully brought with her. She urged the widow not to look into the parcel until she returned three days later.

Thrilled with her luck Doll went further, getting the widow to say prayers in certain parts of the house and making magical play with a pair of scissors. In the course of cavorting round the house, she had a look in the pantry, and before leaving she demanded a turkey and a chicken to take to the Queen of the Fairies.

Doll was so pleased with her success that she could not restrain herself from going back the next day to swindle the old lady out of more of her property, and perhaps also to do what she had been sent for — that is, persuade her to marry Peters. But she was not the only one unable to restrain herself; the widow had looked into the cloth, found the stones and called a constable, who arrested Doll and took her to Newgate Prison.

The story seems to end happily for the widow; but in fact Peters employed other helpers who managed to get Mrs Mescall drunk and he married her in that state, at night, having presumably bribed a parson with no morals at all to conduct the ceremony.

We can follow Doll into gaol, almost,

for a man who was imprisoned a little later wrote about it at great length. His name was William Fennor and he was not a criminal like Ned Browne, but more like one of Browne's victims. He was a young gentleman who came up to London and lost money at the hands of such characters, and was soon in debt to the tune of £100. One day whilst he was taking a walk two sergeants came up to him and one put his hand on his shoulder and said, 'Sir, we arrest you.' They were grisly fellows, one with black, greasy hair and a red nose, the other with a wide mouth, a big nose and a face full of smallpox holes. Sergeants never wore uniform and often disguised themselves to make an arrest, but they always carried a stout truncheon and the subject of their attentions was wise to give up his sword without fuss and go quietly.

Once William Fennor had agreed to go with them, the sergeants stopped menacing him and became quite oily. They begged him not to think they meant him any harm personally, they were only doing their job, and if he was well behaved with them they could help him a lot — get him light treatment in gaol, for instance, possibly arrange bail and even arrange for an easy

58 Mary Frith, the infamous thief, disguised as a man. She was popularly known as Moll Cut-Purse because of her activities as a pick-pocket.

sentence when his case came up. William was now most impressed and fell into their trap — they suggested he might like one last visit to the pub before going to gaol. So he bought the three of them a good meal and lots to drink.

The sergeants, having been fed and wined, became their surly selves once more and hustled William off to a prison in London called the Counter. There a porter was quick to open the gate and soon Fennor was before a man who looked like a gardener, who entered his details in the 'Black Book', and asked him what sort of lodging he would have in prison — the Master's side (which was best but most expensive), the Knights' ward (which was not so nice, but cheaper), the Twopenny ward (which was very cheap and very nasty), or the Hole (where the poorest prisoners were flung to starve unless some City charity paid to support them). Nothing was provided free, it was explained, but he could have things on credit if he had friends who would foot the bill in the end. So Fennor decided on the Master's side and a fat man with a red face and a scrubby beard led him upstairs. There sat a porter who demanded a shilling (5p) to open the door, the first of many such 'fees' that were charged in prison. They went along a gallery into a hall which was nicely and suitably painted with a story of the Prodigal Son, and there the fat man asked for his fee of two shillings (10p). William tried to argue, but it was made quite clear that he would get no bed that night if he did not pay, so he handed over the cash. Upstairs, in a cobwebby room, a pair of very old sheets were put on a bed for him and he was left with a stump of candle to contemplate his companions in the dormitory and the locked door.

The next day his cell mates were curious to know what he was in for and to hear the details of the case. A lawyer offered his services, and said that for a fee of 3s 9d (17p) then and £2 later he could get Fennor out on a writ of *habeas corpus* and have the case removed to the King's Bench, a notoriously shiftless court which would take an age to get into action. But William declined the offer. He knew he had not enough money and he distrusted the lawyer, who must have been crooked if he himself was in prison.

The prisoners strolled about freely, drinking and smoking, and then attended a service. After that came the main meal of the day and a big shock for Fennor — as the newest member of the group he had to pay for wine for everybody. After the meal, the warders came to him and asked for 'garnish', a slang word used then to demand yet more money — sixpence (2½p) this time. Fennor tried to refuse, but they said they would lock him up if he did not comply, so he gave them the last of his ready money — from now on he would have to live on credit.

For three weeks Fennor got away with it, but then the gaolers began to realize he could not pay at this rate, so they moved him to the Knights' ward. There he met a very tall man, like a bean-pole, with what he called a 'chapfallen' face, who demanded 1s 6d (7½p) for his fee. Fennor promised to pay just as soon as he had some ready money, but the warder was angry and put him in a very unsavoury room, just next

door to the lavatory. Tudor drains were bad, and this was a cruel fate.

So Fennor spent much time walking in the yard, occasionally joining a merry gang who lived in a cellar off the yard and seemed always to have a party going, drinking, smoking and singing. Prisoners could have anything if they had the money — they could even go out into London. One clever prisoner persuaded his warder that he could raise money from friends if he could go out. So the warder went with him and they plodded all round London, trying all his friends, but all refused. When they were tired out the prisoner asked as a favour whether he could call at the barber's on his way back to prison to have a much needed trim. As a bribe he offered to pay for the warder to be shaved. The prisoner had his trim and the warder sat in the chair. The barber covered his face with lather and, of course, when he got up the prisoner had escaped.

Eventually, Fennor got out of prison, but not before paying a huge bill, including sixpence (2½p) to the book-keeper for making out his bill and another sixpence (2½p) to the porter for opening the gate. He must have thanked God for his friends, or he would have had to stay in prison for ever, finally descending to the dreaded Hole. As soon as he was free, Fennor wrote down his experiences as a grim warning to others.

59   Supper at an inn.

List of dates

1485 Henry VII comes to the throne.
1509 Henry VIII succeeds.
1514 Miles Coverdale made a priest.
1525 Birth of Thomas Stucley and John Isham.
1528 Miles Coverdale joins William Tyndale. Thomas Whythorne born.
1529 Thomas Wolsey falls. William Grey succeeds to his family title.
1533 Henry VIII marries Anne Boleyn. Elizabeth born.
1535 Miles Coverdale's Bible produced.
1537 Birth of Prince Edward.
1539 Act of Six Articles turns back the course of Reformation in England.
1540 Juan Vives dies.
1544 May, Earl of Hertford invades Scotland.
July, Henry VIII goes to France. September, Boulogne taken.
1545 September, Hertford to Scotland again.
1547 Henry dies and Edward VI becomes king, with Hertford as Protector. In February Hertford was made Duke of Somerset.
1548 April, Haddington taken.
1549 June, the Western Rising. October, Somerset to the Tower; John Dudley, Earl of Warwick, takes control.
1551 Warwick made Duke of Northumberland. Coverdale made Bishop of Exeter.

1552 January, Somerset executed. John Isham marries.
1553 July, Edward dies, Northumberland has his daughter-in-law, Lady Jane Grey, proclaimed Queen. Nine days later Queen Mary takes power, Northumberland executed.
1554 July, Mary marries Philip of Spain.
1555 February, Miles Coverdale escapes.
1558 January, Calais captured. November, Mary dies, Elizabeth succeeds.
1559 Thomas Whythorne to Cambridge. April, Robert Dudley, Earl of Leicester, becomes chief favourite of the Queen. December, attack on Scotland begun.
1560 Robert Carey born.
1562 Shane O'Neill submits and then restarts his rebellion. December, Lord Grey dies.
1564 Merchant Adventurers granted new charter.
1569 January, Miles Coverdale dies.
1571 Lady Hoby born. Thomas Whythorne publishes his songs. October, Battle of Lepanto.
1572 John Isham retires.
1575 March, Elizabeth treats with Spanish governor of the Netherlands and he agrees not to shelter her enemies.
1577 Don Juan's projected attack on England fails.
1578 4 August, Battle of Alcazar.

1587	February, execution of Mary Queen of Scots.
1588	July/August — the Armada.
1591	August, Essex to France to aid Henri of Navarre.
1593	Siege of Rouen.
1595	Judith Phillips charged.
1596	Lady Hoby marries. John Isham and Thomas Whythorne die.
1603	24 March, Queen Elizabeth dies.

Book list

The following were used to find the information for this book:

Brooks, F.W., 'Supplementary Stiffkey Papers', in *Camden Miscellany,* Vol. 16, 1936

Churchyard, T., 'Share in and Eye Witness Accounts of the Seige of Guisness' from A. F. Pollard, *Tudor Tracts,* 1903, pp. 289-301

de Malpas Grey Egerton, Sir P., *A Commentary of the Services of William Lord Grey of Wilton, K.G.,* Camden Society, Old Series, 1847

Ferrers, G., 'The Winning of Calais by the French' from A.F. Pollard, *Tudor Tracts,* 1903, pp. 321-32.

Harrison, G.B., 'Keep the Widow Waking', *Transaction of the Bibliographical Society,* Vol.11, 1930

Judges, A.V., *The Elizabethan Underworld,* 1930

Mares, F.H., *Memoirs of Robert Carey,* Oxford University Press 1972

Meads, D.M., *The Diary of Lady Margaret Hoby,* Boston, 1930

Mozley, J.F., *Coverdale and his Bibles,* 1953, SPCK

Osborn, J.M., *The Autobiography of Thomas Whythorne,* Oxford University Press, 1961

Ramsey, G.D., *John Isham's Accounts, 1558-1572,* Northamptonshire Record Society, 1962

Saunders, H.W., *The Official Papers of Sir Nathaniel Bacon, of Stiffkey, Norfolk, as Justice of the Peace, 1580-1620,* Camden Society, 3rd Series, 1915

Simpson, R., *School of Shakespeare,* 1878

Watson, F., *Tudor School Boy Life,* 1908

Some other books on the Tudor period:

Dodd, A.H., *Life in Elizabethan England,* Batsford, 1961

Doncaster, I., *Elizabethan and Jacobean Home Life,* Longman, 1962

Emmison, F.G., *Tudor Food and Pastimes,* Benn, 1964

Fincham, P., *Tudor Town and Court Life,* Longman, 1969

Harrison, M. and Bryant, M.E., *Picture Source Books for Social History: The Sixteenth Century,* Allen and Unwin, 1951

Harrison, M. and Royston, O.M., *How They Lived: Tudors and Stuarts,* Blackwell, 1963

Neurath, M. and Turner, M., *They Lived Like This in Shakespeare's England,* Macdonald, 1968

Pearce, P., *People of the Past: The Six-teenth Century,* Oxford University Press, 1966

Routh, C.R.N., *They Saw It Happen, 1485-1688,* Blackwell, 1956

Routh, C.R.N., *Who's Who in History, 1485-1603,* Vol.2, Blackwell, 1964

Williams, P., *Life in Tudor England,* Batsford, 1964

In the Longman 'Then and There' series the following are useful:

Bradbury, J., *Shakespeare and His Theatre*
Davies, K., *Henry Percy and Henry VIII*
Donahue, P., *Plymouth Ho! The West in Elizabethan Times*

Fletcher, A.J., *Elizabethan Village*
Goyder, R., *A Reformation Family*
Reeves, M., *Elizabethan Court*
Reeves, M., and Hodgson, P., *Elizabethan Citizen*
Robinson, G., *Elizabethan Ship*

There are a number of 'Jackdaws' on the period:

5 *The Armada;* 9 *Young Shakespeare;* 25 *Henry VIII and the Dissolution of the Monasteries;* 26 *Mary Queen of Scots;* 53 *Elizabeth I;* 54 *Shakespeare's Theatre;* 55 *Cardinal Wolsey;* 56 *Sir Thomas More;* 60 *Hampton Court.*

Index

The numbers in **bold** type refer to the figure numbers of the illustrations

account books, John Isham's, **42, 49**
Alcazar, battle of, 36
ale houses, 11; **57**
America, 32
Ames, Agnes, 9, 10
Antwerp, 38, 51, 52, 54, 55
    Stock Exchange, **45**
apprenticeship, 51
Armada, 11, 25; **13**
armour, 11
army, 11, 25, 30, 35, 43-50

Bacon, Sir Francis, 7, 14; **2, 3**
    Sir Nathaniel, 6-12, 13, 14, 56; **2**
    Sir Nicholas, 14; **1**
Bacon family, 7, 14; **2**
    tree, **2**
bailiwick, 5
Barker, Elizabeth, 53
Barnes, Robert, 37, 38, 40
battles, 33, 36; **24**
Bible, Coverdale's translation, 38; **29**
    other translations of the, 38, 42
    study of the, 37
Boulogne, 41
Brandon, Charles, *see* Suffolk, Duke of
Bromfield, William, 61
Browne, Ned, 63-5
Burghley, William Cecil, Lord, 14,
    27, 30

Calais, 25, 43, 44, 45; **36, 38**
Calvin, John, 40
Cambridge University, 51, 61
cannon, 34
Carey, Robert, *see* Monmouth, Earl of
cargoes, 55; **46**
Carrew, Sir Peter, 19
Catholics, Roman, 12, 16, 33, 37, 38,
    40, 51
Cecil, William, *see* Burghley, Lord
Charles I, 29; **17**
children, 13, 18-21

Chipping Campden, cloth hall and
    wool market, **47**
Churchyard, Thomas, 49, 50
clothes, 18
confidence tricksters, 10, 64-7
Counter Prison, 66
Court, the Tudor, 6, 23-7, 31
courtiers, 23-9
Coverdale, Elizabeth, 40
    Miles, 6, 37-42; **33**
Crane family, 9, 10
crime, 7-11, 63-7
Cromer Pier, 11
Cromwell, Thomas, 38, 40; **27**
Curtis, Thomas, 32
Cut-Purse, Moll, **58**

Dakins, Margaret, *see* Hoby, Lady
    Margaret
debt, 25, 67
Denmark, 41
Devereux, Robert, 13
    Walter, 13-14
diary, Lady Hoby's, 5, 13, 16-17; **6**
diplomacy, 23-6, 28, 31
Dudley, Ambrose, 14, 60
    John, *see* Northumberland,
        Duke of
    Robert, 32
dulcimer, **53**

education, 13, 16, 18-21, 51
Edward VI, 30, 40, 44, 59; **31**
Elizabeth I, 13, 24, 25, 26, 27, 28,
    32, 33, 42, 50, 51; **16**
Essex, Earl of, 13
exports, 52

Ferrour, John, 10
Fleet Prison, 11
Flower, Joan, **4**
    Margaret, **4**
    Phillipa, **4**

flute, **53**
food, 20, 21
forts, 38
France, 25, 30, 31
    war with, 43-50
Frith, Mary, **58**

gallows, 65
games, 21; **11**
Geneva, 42
Gray's Inn, London, 7
Grey, Arthur, 47, 49
    Jane, Lady, 59
    William, Lord, 6, 43-50; **41**
Guise, Duke of, 49, 50; **39**
Guisnes, 43, 44, 45
    siege of, 45-50

Hackness estate, 13-17
Hamburg, 38
Hampton Court, 26; **12**
harpsichord, 62
Henry VIII, 40, 43, 44
Henry of Navarre, 25
Hertford, Earl of, *see* Somerset,
    Duke of
Heywood, John, 57
Hoby, Lady Margaret, 5, 13-17
    Sir Thomas Posthumous, 14-17
holidays, 21
homework, 21
household management, 13, 16
Huntingdon, Catherine, Countess of,
    13, 14, 16

imports, 52-3, 54
inn, **59**
Ireland, 32, 33
Isham, Elizabeth, 53
    John, 51-6; **49**
Isham family, 51-6

James I, 24, 26, 28

Jesuits, 6, 12
Juan, Don, of Austria, 33, 34; **25**
Justices of the Peace, 7, 10-12, 13, 56

Kerr, Sir Robert, 26

Laborne, Henry, 10
Lamport Manor, 55, 56
languages, 18-19
Latimer, Bishop, **31**
Latin, 18, 19, 21, 37
law and order, 7, 9, 10, 11
Lepanto, battle of, 33; **24**
Lisbon, 35; **26**
loans (money), 10, 11, 54-5
London, 7, 11, 12, 14, 32, 38, 40, 54, 56, 57, 61
    Tower of, 31, 45; **21**
lute, 57; **53**

Macalpine, Agnes, 40
    John, 40
madrigals, 61
Magdalen College School, Oxford, 57
Marches, 23, 25, 26, 28, 44
marriage, 13, 25
marriage-broker, 62
Mary, Queen of Scots, 24
Mary I, 32, 41, 42, 45, 51; **37**
meals, 17, 21, 56
Mercers' Hall, London, 51, 56; **43**
Middle Temple, London, 51, 54
money lenders, 10, 54-5
Monmouth, Robert Carey, Earl of, 6, 14, 23-9, 44; **18**
monopolies, 11
Montreuil, siege of, 43
mortars, **40**
Mower, Elizabeth, 9, 10
Murchieson, Agnes, 40
    Elizabeth, 40
music, 21, 57, 61, 62
music-making, **52, 53**
muster, 11

navy, 11, 25, 33
Netherlands, 23, 59
Newgate Prison, 65

Nonsuch Palace, **15**
Norfolk, 7, 11
Northumberland, John Dudley, Duke of, 30, 45, 59, 60

O'Neill, Shane, 32, 33
Oxford University, 57

parents, 18, 19
Paris, 23
Parliament, Members of, 7, 12, 16, 51
Parris, George van, 40-1
patents, 11
pens, to make, 20
Philip II, 33, 45, 49; **23, 37**
Phillips, Doll, 65
    Judith, 65
pickpocketing, 19
piracy, 30, 32
plague, 42, 61
Poor Law, 11
Pope, Doll, 65
Pope, the, 10, 33, 34, 35
Portugal, 35-6
    king of, 35, 36
prayers, family, **8**
prisons, 11, 65, 66-7
Protestants, 12, 13, 16, 37-42
Puritans, 13, 16
purses, cutting of, 63

rebellion of 1549, 41
religion, 6, 12, 37-42
rogues and vagabonds, 63
Rome, 33, 34
Romero, Julian, 30
Rouen, siege of, 25; **14**
Russell, Lady Elizabeth, 14, 51; **7**

sailors, 7, 11, 63
school fees, 18
schools, 18-21, 57; **9, 10**
Scotland, 24, 25, 26, 28, 44, 50
sea defences, 11
servants, 16, 18, 60
Seymour, Edward, *see* Somerset, Duke of
sheriffs, 7, 12, 56
shipwrecks, 11, 55

Sidney, Sir Henry, Lord Deputy of Ireland, 33
    Sir Philip, 14
    Thomas, 14-15
sieges, 24, 25, 43, 45-50; **14, 35**
Sluys, siege of, 24
soldiers, 11, 30, 48, 63
Somerset, Edward Seymour, Duke of, 6, 30, 44, 45; **20**
sorcery, 10
Spain, 33, 49, 55
    war with, 25; **13**
Stuart, Mary, 33, 34
Stucley, Sir Thomas, 5, 6, 30-6
Suffolk, Charles Brandon, Duke of, 30; **19**

taxes, 11
teachers, 18, 19, 20, 57, 61; **9, 10**
toys, **11**
trade, 11, 51-6
    cloth, 51, 52, 54, 55
tutors, *see* teachers
Tyndale, William, 38; **28**

Ulster, 33; **22**
unemployment, 63
universities, 18, 51, 57, 61
Upton, priest, 12

vestments, 42; **32**
Veysey, Bishop, 14
virginals, 54, 57, 58
Vives, Juan Luis, 18

Watts, Thomas, 10
weapons, 11, 43, 47, 49; **34, 40**
weaving, **48**
Whythorne, Thomas, 5, 6, 13-14, 57-62; **51, 54**
Whythorne family, 57
wife-stealing, 9
witches and witchcraft, 9, 10; **4**
Woodhouse, Francis, 12
Wotton, Mr, 19
writing, 20; **6, 30**
Wymondham, 10

Yorkshire, 13, 17